D0860986

Other Kaplan Books for 8th Graders:

High School 411

Grammar Power

Learning Power

Reading Power

No-Stress Guide to the New York State 8th Grade Tests

Second Edition

Cynthia and Drew Johnson

Simon & Schuster

SYDNEY · LONDON · SINGAPORE · NEW YORK · TORONTO

Kaplan Publishing
Published by Simon & Schuster
1230 Avenue of the Americas
New York, NY 10020

Copyright © 2001 by Anaxos Inc.

Illustrations Copyright © by Dave Chipps

All rights reserved. No part of this book may be reproduced or transmitted in any form or by any means, electronic or mechanical, including photocopying, recording, or by any information storage and retrieval system, without the written permission of the Publisher, except where permitted by law.

Kaplan® is a registered trademark of Kaplan, Inc.

For bulk sales to schools, please contact: Order Department, Simon & Schuster, 100 Front Street, Riverside, NJ 08075. Phone: 1-800-223-2336. Fax: 1-800-943-9831.

The material in this book is up-to-date at the time of publication. However, changes may have been instituted in the test after this book was published.

Project Editor: Ruth Baygell

Contributing Editors: Marc Bernstein, Marcy Bullmaster, Phillip Vlahakis

Cover Design: Cheung Tai

Interior Page Design and Layout: Laurel Douglas

Production Editor: Maude Spekes

Executive Editor: Del Franz

Manufactured in the United States of America

September 2001

10 9 8 7 6 5 4 3 2 1

ISBN: 0-7432-1413-7

All of the practice questions in this book were created by the authors to illustrate question types. They are not actual test questions. For additional information on the New York State 8th Grade Tests, visit the New York State Education Department Web site at www.nysed.gov.

Contents

Introduction: Welcome to the New York State 8th Grade Tests 1

Chapter 1: Test-Taking Strategies 7

Chapter 2: Mathematics. 17

    Sample Questions: Mathematics. 42

Chapter 3: English Language Arts 47

    Sample Questions: English Language Arts 72

Chapter 4: English Language Arts: Composition 79

Chapter 5: Science and Technology Assessment 91

Chapter 6: Social Studies 107

Chapter 7: Epilogue 115

Answer Key: Sample Questions. 119

Authors

Cynthia Johnson is the author of several educational books for young people, including *Word Smart Junior* and *Writing Smart Junior*, both of which received the prestigious Parent's Choice Gold Award in 1995, and were included in *Curriculum Administrator* magazine's list of "Top 100" educational products for 1996.

Drew Johnson is the author of *Kidding Around Austin!*, a travel activity book for children, and coauthor of *Kaplan Learning Power*, a guide to improving study skills. Drew is currently an education writer and editor creating workbook, textbook, and World Wide Web–based educational materials for students of all ages.

Welcome to the New York State 8th Grade Tests

> The following manuscript has been translated into English from its original language, Kronhorsti, an alien language spoken by the inhabitants of the fourth planet orbiting the sun Cygnus X-7.
>
> —X!Frumious

TO: The Most Supreme Ruler of the Planet Kronhorst

FROM: X!Frumious the Explorer, currently stationed on Earth

RE: The discovery of standardized tests within the universe

Dear Most Grand Leader of Kronhorst,

Greetings from Earth! As you know, my team of explorers and I have been spending some time on this planet to learn more about its culture and people. For the most part, I can tell you that human beings are intelligent, kind, and helpful, unless you happen to be driving too slow in the left lane of the highway; then, it's a WHOLE different story, and not one I can tell you with the interplanetary censors around. It is interesting to note that, like every other species we have encountered in the universe, humans have invented the sport which we know as **clickvellsgerstoof** and which they call "professional wrestling." There is, however, one thing that humans have invented that exists nowhere else in known space—standardized testing.

Eager to learn all we could about standardized tests, my crew and I looked for a place on Earth to land. Almost everyone I talked to warned me that once the Earthlings saw my crew and me, they would run screaming from our bizarre appearance—but when we landed in Manhattan's East Village, no such thing occurred (although I did lose 20 human dollars on something called a "card game.")

Lucky for us we landed in New York, because once there we discovered some standardized tests known as the New York State 8th Grade exams. We soon learned that these tests were first given in 1999 as the focal point of a new, tougher set of academic standards set forth by Education Commissioner Richard Mills. Mr. Mills made testing at all grade levels the focal point of his agenda, toughening the academic standards and changing the format of the test to a multiple-day, diverse-question set-up.

Here's a brief description of the tests:

Overview: 8th Grade New York State Tests

English Language Arts: *Two 90-minute sessions*

Session 1
- Read 4 passages and answer 25 mulitiple-choice questions
- Listen to a passage and write 3 short responses and 1 extended response

Session 2
- Read 2 related passages and write 3 short responses and 1 extended response
- Write a composition

Mathematics: *Two 70-minute sessions*

Session 1
- Answer 27 multiple-choice questions
- Answer 4 short-response and 2 extended-response questions

Session 2
- Answer 8 short-response and 4 extended-response questions

Science*: *Two sessions*

Session 1
- Answer roughly 45 multiple-choice and open-ended questions (2 hours)

Session 2
- Perform various scientific procedures at three lab stations (1 hour)

Social Studies*: *Two 90-minute sessions*

Session 1
- Answer 45 multiple-choice and 3 or 4 extended-response questions

Session 2
- Answer 1 document-based question

Technology Assessment*: *One 90-minute session*

- Answer about 40 multiple-choice and 10 extended response questions

*Debuted in 2001

Scoring

For the ELA and Math exams, you will receive a final score of 1 (deficient) through 4 (advanced). Scoring methods for the Science, Social Studies, and Technology Assessment exams were not finalized at the time of publication.

On multiple-choice questions, you'll receive credit only for those questions that you answer correctly. On open-ended questions, you can receive partial credit.

There is no penalty for wrong answers, and an answer left blank receives no credit.

Calculators

Not permitted on multiple-choice section but required for rest of math test.

So as you can see, O Great Ruler, the New York State tests are much harder than the typical Kronhorsti test, and the students have fewer brains to help them.

In the spirit of pioneering, I, X!Frumious the Explorer, decided to become the first Kronhorstian to take and pass the 8th Grade tests. I put on the regulation human disguise–these Earthlings have only two legs, how can they dance?–and enrolled at Eastbury High School in Albany. I made some mistakes on the first day I was in school, such as eating a cafeteria bench, but soon I fit right in with the rest of the student body. However, after attending some classes, I realized that having a high-school degree from a distant planet doesn't mean you can pass an eighth-grade standardized test.

KAPLAN

You see, the 8th Grade Tests were designed by the **New York State Education Department** (NYSED) to see how well students were mastering the state's curriculum. The exams provide a way for NYSED to determine whether or not a student has mastered the skill objectives for his or her grade level.

It's a good arrangement, but it meant I was going to need human help if I wanted to pass the tests. Fortunately, I found four Eastbury students who asked me to join their study group. It turns out that the phrase "study group" means the same thing in English as it does in Kronhorsti, except in a human study group there's no major surgery involved. This study group already had people who were specialists in the different test-taking areas, but they needed someone to take notes. I eagerly volunteered to be the study group note taker, and everyone was happy.

The members of my study group are:

Daniel Bryant, who specializes in test-taking strategies. He'll also lead our social studies section

Ridley Anderson, an expert at mathematics

Angela Lupino, the English language arts guru

William Walker, also known as "Willy H_2SO_4," who is in charge of the essay and science sections.

And of course there is me, **X!Frumious**, the group recorder.

O Exalted Ruler, I have provided the notes of our study group meetings on the following pages so that you might learn as much about the 8th Grade tests as I have. I have also included testlike questions throughout this book so you can try out your skills on sample problems. It's my belief that anyone who learns the techniques discussed in this book and goes on to use them on the exams will be able to pass these tests, regardless of what planet he or she originally came from.

I Remain Your Humble Citizen,

X!Frumious

X!Frumious the Explorer, of the planet Kronhorst

Test-Taking Strategies

Session Leader: Daniel Bryant

O Most Mighty One, here are the notes from my first study group meeting. Whenever Daniel wrote something down on the blackboard, I have included that drawing among my notes.
—X!Frumious

NAME: Daniel J. Bryant

BORN: May 22, 1989
Wallkill, New York

NOTES: Daniel actually likes standardized tests, which puts him in the same category as about one half of one percent of American students. He took the SAT at age 12 for the first time as part of a Duke University study, and he hopes to turn a good score on the PSAT test into a National Honor Society Scholarship to college. Daniel owns one dog, a Malamute named Abacab.

Daniel:	First, I'd like to thank everyone for showing up to the meeting on time. Before we start, I asked X!Frumious to go to the store and get us some snacks for the group. How did that go, X!Frumy?
X!Frumious:	Just fine. I was walking down the aisle with barbecue and picnic supplies and I found these delightful items. They really taste great.
Daniel:	X!Frumious, that's charcoal. You're eating gasoline-soaked briquettes.
Ridley:	Let's just skip the snacks for now. Agreed?
Daniel:	Good. Now, down to business. In order to succeed on the 8th Grade New York State tests, there are several strategies you need to master. The first one sounds simple, but it's crucial: Get to know the format of the test inside and out. This means you should know how many multiple-choice questions are in each section, when you can use your calculator and when you can't, and how much time you have for each section.
Willy:	Why is this important? We've all taken some form of a standardized test before.
Daniel:	That might be true, but knowing exactly what's ahead will help you relieve some uncertainty about the test. You'll go into the test with a better frame of mind.

Let's face it, there's a lot of pressure to do well on these tests. The normal human reaction is to feel nervous and anxious. The problem is, feeling nervous or anxious while taking a test almost always leads to a lower score. Granted, I don't expect you to be excited about the New York State tests, but you do need familiarize yourself with what you'll be tested on, so you can do the best you can.

Ridley: So Familiarity = Confidence on the tests?

Daniel: Right. It gives you confidence *before* and *during* the test. We all know people who have suffered from "test meltdown," where they freak out over a question they just can't understand. While you can't prevent coming across a question that stumps you, you can learn the best way to handle the situation. How you handle yourself during a test is almost as important as knowing how to answer a question.

> ### Strategy 1
> Understand the format of the test like the back of your hand.

Willy: I'll need an example before I agree with your theory.

Daniel: On one part of the English Language Arts (ELA) test, you listen to a story and then answer questions about what you heard. If you aren't prepared beforehand for this unusual format, you would have to spend time figuring out what to do during the test.

Now, the next test-taking strategy you all must learn is the concept of pacing.

Setting a steady, consistent pace on each test section is an essential part of doing well. This means you never rush through a question and make a hurried mistake, but you also don't spend too long on a tough question and then miss the opportunity to answer the easy questions behind it. Also, since these

> ### Strategy 2
> Maintain a consistent pace throughout the test. Don't rush through any one question. Even if you think you can answer a question in 10 seconds, remember that the test is designed to challenge you, so seemingly obvious answers may not be what you think. Similarly, don't spend too much time on a question. If you do, you might become drained and lose the focus you need to solve the remaining problems.

tests are administered over a period of days, don't exhaust yourself on the first day of testing.

Spend at least a minute on each question—if you go faster you may make a careless error—but never spend too long on any one question. No single question is critical to your overall test score, so if you are having trouble with a problem, don't get bent out of shape about it. The best way to approach every section is to use a *two-pass system*. Go through each test section twice. First, complete the easy problems. Then go back and work through the more difficult ones.

Strategy 3

Use a two-pass system on each section of the test.

- *First, go through and answer all the questions you're comfortable with.*

- *Then, go back and spend more time on the harder questions. This means leaving the extended-response questions until the end.*

Willy: Why should I spend at least a minute on every question if I can figure it out in seconds?

Daniel: Because the test is designed to challenge you, so there are lots of traps to trip you up. For instance, there are misleading —but wrong—answer choices that you might pick if you're in a hurry. Here's an example:

1. A teacher is making 7 walking sticks for use in the school play. If each stick requires $3\frac{3}{4}$ feet of wood, how much wood is needed altogether for the 7 sticks?

    A. $10\frac{3}{4}$

    B. $17\frac{1}{2}$

    C. $21\frac{3}{4}$

    D. $26\frac{1}{4}$

If you didn't take the time to work out the math here, you might be tempted by A or C, since both have $\frac{3}{4}$ in them—similar to the $3\frac{3}{4}$ in the original problem. C looks especially good because at first glance 7 multiplied by $3\frac{3}{4}$ equals $21\frac{3}{4}$.

Ridley: However, if you took a minute to do the math, you would see that $3\frac{3}{4}$ times 7 is really $26\frac{1}{4}$, choice D. Initially, this didn't appear a likely answer, but if you work through the math, it is correct.

> **Strategy 4**
>
> *Answer every question, even if you need to guess. There's no penalty for wrong answers, so any question you skip is a missed opportunity for free points.*

Daniel: Let's say you've gone through the first pass, and you're on the second pass, working on a tougher problem. You spend about five minutes looking it over, but you still don't know how to answer it. Do you leave it blank and move on? The answer is, No, No, No!!

You won't lose points for getting a question wrong, so even if you have only a one in four chance of answering correctly, make sure to bubble in an oval on the answer grid. Any question you skip is a missed opportunity for free points.

> **Strategy 5**
>
> *On multiple-choice questions, use the **Process of Elimination** (POE) to eliminate wrong answer choices. Every wrong answer choice you rule out helps you to narrow down the number of choices you must select from.*

Willy: Sounds fine, but if we have only a one in four chance on a question, we won't get many questions right with those odds.

Daniel: That's true, but the next strategy will help you improve those odds. The technique is called *Process of Elimination*, or *POE*, and it's an effective tool for ruling out incorrect answer choices on multiple-choice questions.

Remember, the answer to every multiple-choice question is right in front of you. You aren't expected to know an answer off the top of your head, you just have to be able to select the correct answer from a list of choices. That means that getting rid of wrong answers is just as useful as finding the correct answer, because every wrong answer choice you rule out brings you closer to getting the problem right. Here's an example of how POE can be effective.

Daniel holds up his right hand clenched in a fist.

O Mighty Leader, remember your plans to shrink the Statue of Liberty to the size of a peanut? Please cancel those plans; something just came up.

2. What am I holding in my hand?

A. a subway train
B. a penny
C. the Statue of Liberty
D. an eraser

Which answer choices can you eliminate?

Angela: A and C, because your hand isn't big enough to hold a subway train or the Statue of Liberty. Common sense tells me it has to be something much smaller than those two choices.

Daniel: Most observant. So the answer is either B or D. There's no way to know which is correct, but having a 50/50 chance on a series of test questions means you're bound to get some questions right just by guessing.

Watch out for traps, though. Many math questions will slip in answer choices that contain numbers from the original question, or that use numbers from the question in a simplified way.

3. Kerry and her mother used 45 feet of rope from a 60-yard bundle of rope. How many feet of rope were left in the bundle?

A. 15 feet
B. 60 feet
C. 105 feet
D. 135 feet

Before doing the math, B contains a number from the problem itself (a trap!), and can most likely be eliminated. If you rush on this problem, you might pick A or C, since these answers just add or subtract the two numbers in the question. However, if you look closely, you'll see that Kerry and her mother have taken 45 *feet* from a 60 *yard* bundle. That means choice A is definitely not correct. At this point you can guess between C or D if you can't figure out how to do the math, but since C is probably a trap, D is your best bet. And it's the right answer.

Angela: But what about the math?

Ridley: Oh, that's easy, you just take 60 yards and multiply by three, so that . . .

Daniel: Ridley could explain the math correctly, Angela, but she doesn't have to, because we already have the answer, D. This is the advantage of the multiple-choice format; it doesn't matter how you get the right answer, so long as you bubble in the correct oval. So whether you do the math or use elimination to pick choice D, you get the same amount of credit.

Of course, you can't use elimination on every test question. In fact, the open-response problems are designed specifically to prevent you from using it.

> ### Strategy 6
>
> *Use common sense to think about what the answer to a question could be. It sounds simple, and it is, but under high-stakes tests conditions, many students panic and forget certain basics. Look for traps that might appear in the question.*

Willy: Does POE work well on English Language Arts?

Daniel: Yes. For instance, in the ELA sections, some wrong answer choices are words taken directly from the reading passage. These words have nothing to do with the question being asked, but since you might remember having read them in the passage, those answer choices seem to be correct, or at least reasonable. Consider the following question:

4. Which is a FACT in the passage?

   A. The teachers mentioned in the program are distinguished.
   B. The postal service is very slow.
   C. The skills test will not affect admission into the school.
   D. The school library is open 24 hours a day.

Using common sense, which answer choices can you eliminate?

Ridley: I'd get rid of D, since I've never heard of a school library that is open 24 hours a day.

Daniel: True. You can bet, however, that the "school library" is mentioned at least once in the passage, so someone else might not cross out D because he or she remembers reading those words in the passage.

Angela: Choice B doesn't seem like a good choice, either. It is such a broad statement that it would be hard to prove as fact, which is what the question is asking. I would eliminate it as well.

Daniel: Good. That leaves A and C, and since A is a general statement that could be hard to prove as fact, I'd pick C. As it happens, C is correct.

Using only POE, we were able to get the answer, and we never laid eyes on the passage itself.

POE works just as well on Science, Technology, and Social Studies. Check out the following question.

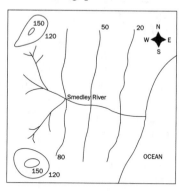

5. According to the topographic map, the Smedley River flows in what direction?

    A. north
    B. south
    C. east
    D. west

You don't need to be a riverologist—or whatever you call someone who knows about rivers—in order to get this problem right. You just need to look at the map and use some common sense. For instance, the Smedley River crosses the map in a fairly straight line, so what choices can we eliminate first?

Willy: North and south, choices A and B. I can see with my eyes that the river is not going in either of those directions.

Daniel: Exactly. So now, you could either guess or look at the elevation numbers on the map. The higher numbers are on the left side of the page, and since I know water flows downhill, C is the right answer.

Angela: I got C, too, but that's just because I used common sense and knew that rivers always flow into the ocean, not the other way around. So the answer had to be C.

Daniel: You see, you don't always need to know the exact scientific principle —often a basic understanding of things will be enough. Here, you needed to know how water works.

For the Social Studies exam, elimination is useful too, but in a more limited way—since many of the questions require specific knowledge of history. I'll talk more about this later.

Now, on to the next strategy: Write all of your work down. If you try to solve a problem in your head, you're more likely to make a mistake. If it's written down, you'll be able to retrace your steps.

You'd be surprised how many students don't this; they think they can breeze through problems by doing the math in their heads or by punching in numbers on the calculator—without writing their work down on paper.

Even though you'll have a calculator to help you answer all the open-ended problems, you should still write down the numbers on paper first. Why? Because you need to look at your work and determine

> **Information**
>
> *On the math test, calculators are permitted for all open-ended questions, but not for multiple-choice questions.*

whether you have set up each problem correctly. Do the two numbers need to be multiplied, or is division required? If you just start crunching numbers on your calculator, you could make a careless error.

Ridley: What if the answer is just staring right at me?

Daniel: Then I'd check whether it really is the correct answer, or whether it's just an attractive *wrong* answer. Think back to the "Bundle of Rope" question we discussed earlier. Choices A and C both initially looked like

> **Strategy 7**
>
> *Write all of your work down. You will always want to have your notes to refer to, either to catch a mistake or to double check your work. Don't just work out problems in your head—it isn't worth the risk.*

good choices, but when you did the math, you found out that they both were incorrect.

Writing down your work is crucial on the open-ended math questions. To illustrate this, read the following simplified example:

> Jonathan had $5.00 at the start of the day. At noon, he gave half of his money to Gwendolyn, and at 3:00 p.m. he lost $0.50 in a vending machine. How much money did Jonathan have at the end of the day? Explain your answer.

Imperious Student A: Jonathan had two bucks because I say he did. Now all must bow to the brilliance of Student A!

Well-Behaved Student B: Starting out with five, Jonathan gave half, or $2.50 away, so he had three dollars left. Then he lost 50 cents, so $3.00 − $0.50 = $2.50.

Student A provided the right solution with an inadequate explanation, earning only 1 point out of 2. Student B provided the wrong solution but the right explanation, and that earns 1 point as well. There are 18 open-ended questions on the math test that account for the majority of your math score. Even if you come up with the wrong solution, you'll earn partial credit if you properly show your work.

X!Frumious: Writing everything down is a very good idea.

Daniel: The last strategy is not a strategy in the typical sense—it's about helping you make the most of your time. If you find yourself getting mentally tired during the test—and that's bound to happen—take a moment to stretch and clear your mind. Even though you might be losing a minute or two to rest, you'll actually gain much more than that in the end.

One more thing. While these strategies can help mentally prepare you for the test, there are some physical preparations you should make as well.

What to Do Right Before the Test

Strategy 8

Take short breaks during the test to help you relieve mental fatigue. If you feel yourself getting mentally tired, just put your pencil down and take a minute to stretch. Stretch your arms, stretch your fingers, clear your mind, and then refocus your thoughts back on the test.

- On the night before the test, make sure you get enough sleep. Don't go to bed earlier than usual, however. If you do that, you'll probably just lie in bed thinking about the test.

- Don't cram for the test. Do a light review and then do something to take your mind off it.

- On the day of the test, make sure you have a good breakfast, but not so filling that you find yourself dying for a nap.

- On the day of the test, don't take any over-the-counter medication if you don't have to. Having allergies is annoying, but taking medication that muddles your thinking spells trouble for your test score.

Mathematics

Session Leader: Ridley Anderson

O Munificent Big Guy, what follows are my notes from our second study group meeting, held at the most magnificent place I have ever been in. The place was called a "rec room," and this incredible establishment was located in the basement of Ridley's house, probably for security reasons. I'll tell you more about this place, O Scaly One, when we meet in person.
—X!Frumious

NAME: Ridley L. Anderson

BORN: March 9, 1989
Skaneateles, New York

NOTES: Ridley was voted Head Cheerleader two years in a row, during which time she instituted a policy of issuing jerseys and numbers to cheerleaders in order to "impose a system of order upon this chaos of pom-poms and hair spray." She then resigned as cheerleader in order to start a mathematics club, and was voted President of Math Club three days later. Ridley owns one pet, a mongoose named Euclid.

Ridley: Hello, thank you for all arriving on time today. I know some people find it hard to follow simple directions like "Meet at my house at sixteen seconds past 4:08 p.m."

Daniel: Yes, well, I'd like to take the credit for our punctuality, but we did just follow you home from school. Remember, you said, "Just follow my Mom's car?"

Ridley: Still, it's the thought that counts. Now, my discussion of the math section will take 34 minutes, 8 seconds. I'd appreciate it, X!Frumious, if you would use a watch and notify me at 4 minute, 16 second intervals. Here's a digital watch for you to use. No, X!Frumious, don't eat it.

The Math test is broken up into two sessions. In Session 1, you'll start off by answering 27 multiple-choice questions for 35 minutes, and you'll finish up by switching to open-ended questions (called *short-* and *extended-response*). In session 2, you'll continue on with more open-ended questions. It's interesting to note, however, that the 27 multiple-choice questions account for 39% of your total math score.

Overview: NYS 8th Grade Math Test

Session 1

Part 1 *(35 minutes)*	• *27 multiple-choice questions (1 point)*
Part 2 *(35 minutes)*	• *4 short-response questions (0–2 points)*
	• *2 extended-response questions (0–3 points)*

Session 2 *(70 minutes)* • *8 short-response questions (0–2 points)*

• *4 extended-response questions (0–3 points)*

Scoring — *You will receive an overall score of 1 (deficient) through 4 (advanced). Your score is based on the number of questions that you answer correctly. On open-ended questions, you can receive partial credit. You are not penalized for wrong answers.*

Calculators — *Not permitted on multiple-choice section but required for rest of test.*

Daniel: So about two-fifths of my math score is determined in the first 35 minutes?

Ridley: Yes. In fact, Session 1 counts for about 60% of your math score, while Session 2 accounts for the rest. The entire second day of this test, when we're all slugging through the open-ended questions, is worth as much to our score as the multiple-choice questions we answered earlier.

In other words, about 40% of all the math answers will be sitting in front of you, and all you have to do is pick out the correct answer.

Information

A perfect score on the Math test would be 69 points:

• *27 multiple-choice questions worth 1 point each;*

• *12 short-response questions worth 0–2 points each; and*

• *6 extended-response questions worth 0–3 points each.*

Angela: So it would be helpful to spend more time on the multiple-choice questions than on the open-ended questions.

Ridley: It would be better, Angela, but the test format doesn't allow us to do that. Since Session 1 is broken into two parts, we have only 35 minutes for the 27 multiple-choice questions. This means you'll have only about one minute for each question, so in order to get through all the questions, you must keep a steady pace. Don't let yourself get bogged down for five minutes on one question at the expense of the rest of the section. Fortunately, the test-taking strategies that we'll discuss here work best on multiple-choice questions.

As for the open-ended questions, I'd suggest you spend roughly 5 minutes on each short response, and about 8 minutes on each extended response. The problem is, there's no way to know exactly which questions are worth 2 points and which are worth 3 points. You can kind of figure out which ones are harder—some questions have three parts to them, so you can assume these are worth 3 points. But rather than speculate on how much each question is worth, just remember this: *Spend about 4 minutes— but never more than 8 minutes—on every open-ended question.*

> **Strategy**
>
> On open-ended questions, plan to spend between 4–8 minutes on each. Make sure to show your work, and give every question your best shot using sound math skills.

Willy: That makes sense. I wouldn't want to use up a ton of time on a problem that's worth only 2 points.

Ridley: You've got that right, Willy. Now while the multiple-choice section is scored by a machine, the 2- and 3-point questions are scored by teachers who have been given guidelines about what constitutes a complete response. To get full credit on a 2-point question, you have to show adequate work demonstrating you used proper math skills. If you have the correct solution without any explanation, you'll get 1 point. And if you come up with the *wrong* solution but demonstrate a "mathematically appropriate process," you'll earn 1 point. Now you can see why it's so important to show your work.

Angela: What if I have no clue how to answer a 3-point question?

Ridley: If it's a hard question for you, it's probably tough for a lot of people taking the test. Just move on and answer the other questions. Then, check your answers on the other problems to make sure you haven't made any careless errors. If you still have time, go back to that tough question and give it your best shot. Remember, though, that it won't make or break your score.

Now, I'll discuss each of the Objectives, or Key Ideas, that make up this test. Everybody Ready? X!Frumious, how am I doing for time?

Information

The 8th Grade Math test is designed by the New York State Education Department (NYSED) to see how well students have mastered the state's math curriculum. There are seven test objectives designed to match this curriculum.

X!Frumious: (*mumbled because of something in mouth*) Delicious!

Ridley: Okay then, here we go.

Overview: Math Test Objectives

Key Idea	Description
1. **Mathematical Reasoning** (10–15% of test)	basic word problems that require simple addition, subtraction, multiplication, and division to figure out an unknown quantity
2. **Numbers and Numeration** (10–15% of test)	basic math terminology, such as fractions, whole numbers, and ratios
3. **Operations** (15–20% of test)	problem solving using addition, subtraction, multiplication, and division; order of operations questions; application of various math properties
4. **Modeling/ Multiple Representation** (15–20% of test)	geometric shapes and concepts; use of maps and scale; coordinate plane problems
5. **Measurement** (10–20% of test)	graphs and charts; measurements and concepts related to volume, perimeter, and circumference
6. **Uncertainty** (5–10% of test)	estimation and probability questions
7. **Patterns/Functions** (20–25% of test)	basic math patterns; linear equations, and the Pythagorean theorem

Key Ideas

Key Idea 1: Mathematical Reasoning

Ridley: Math Reasoning can be like basic algebra, since these questions often ask you to identify the value of a "missing number." For instance, a person might start out with 50 apples, but then gain 23 and lose 4, and you are asked to determine how many apples are left. Other Math Reasoning questions require you to use math to draw conclusions, like the following question:

1. Terrence is thinking of a number greater than 150 and less than 200, and Juanita has to guess it. He has provided Juanita with the following clue—the number is divisible by 2, 3, and 5. What number is Terrence thinking of?

   A. 150
   B. 160
   C. 180
   D. 195

Use Process of Elimination to solve this problem. Take one clue at a time, and check the answer choices to see what you can eliminate.

Angela: First, you can get rid of A, since the number has to be *greater than* 150. Then, 195 (Choice D), is not divisible by 2, so that's the next to go. Choice B is not divisible by 3, so that leaves C.

Ridley: C is the answer, then. It's important to take math problems step-by-step. If you don't, you'll likely find them overwhelming. Here's a more difficult Math Reasoning question.

2. The variables q, x, y, and z each represent a different whole number. If you know that $q = 4$, use the properties of whole numbers to determine the numerical value for each of the remaining variables. Show all of your work.

$$q \times y = q$$
$$z + 2y = q$$
$$z \times x = x$$
$$y + y = z$$

$x =$ $\qquad$ $y =$ $\qquad$ $z =$

Daniel: There are three parts to this question, so I'm guessing it's worth 3 points.

Ridley: While I can't confirm or deny this, I agree with you. Since it seems to be an extended-response question, you might want to hold off and do it later. The problem looks tough because it has three unknown variables and four equations, but if you break it down, it becomes simple. Look at the first equation, $q \times y = q$. Since we know $q = 4$, what number does y have to be?

Willy: It would have to be 1, since any number multiplied by 1 is that number.

Ridley: Right. From there, we can use the fourth equation to figure out z, and z has to be 2. At this point, if I've shown my work, I've solved for two of the three unknown variables and

> **Strategy**
>
> On all Mathematical Reasoning problems—and throughout the math test on the whole—break up each multistep question into a series of small steps.

have probably earned 2 points. To earn the full 3 points, I would need to see the third equation, $z \times x = x$, and figure out that $x = 0$, since that's the only number that fits.

Key Idea 2: Numbers and Numerations

Ridley: These questions test your understanding of such basic math principles as whole numbers, integers, even/odd numbers, decimals, fractions, ratios, and percents. What makes these concepts difficult is how they are presented on the test. Consider the following question.

3. Kaitlyn surveyed a group of people at the mall and asked each person what his or her favorite sport was. The chart below shows the result of her survey. Which list shows the results in order from greatest interest to least interest?

Favorite Sport	Part of Group Surveyed
Soccer	$\frac{1}{10}$
Football	$\frac{9}{20}$
Basketball	$\frac{1}{5}$
Baseball	$\frac{1}{4}$

A.   Soccer, Basketball, Baseball, Football
B.   Basketball, Soccer, Football, Baseball
C.   Football, Baseball, Basketball, Soccer
D.   Football, Basketball, Baseball, Soccer

This question is interesting because it combines two different number concepts—*fractions* and *greatest to least*. To solve, let's see which sport is the most popular. The best way to do this is to find a *common denominator* for all the fractions.

Information

To find the common denominator (the denominator is the lower half of a fraction), multiply the numerator and denominator of the Soccer fraction by 2, the numerator and denominator of the Basketball fraction by 4, and the numerator and denominator of the Baseball fraction by 5. That way, all the fractions will have a denominator of 20, the common denominator.

Willy: Once we do that, we see that $\frac{9}{20}$ is the largest fraction there. So, since football is the most popular, I'll eliminate any answer choice that doesn't start with Football. That leaves C and D.

Ridley: Which one has more fans, Baseball or Basketball? Now that we have done the math, we can see that Baseball is the answer ($\frac{5}{20}$ is greater than Basketball's $\frac{4}{20}$) so we can pick C and move on.

Remember that most of the problems on the test are designed to be challenging. On question 3, if you got flustered by the chart format and the talk about sports, knowing how to get a common denominator would not have mattered. If you stay calm and take the time to figure out just what the question is asking, you'll do fine.

Sometimes POE and a healthy dose of common sense are all that you will need to answer these Number Sense questions.

4. Due to increased demand, a car dealership recently raised the price on its new convertibles by 36%. If the original cost of a convertible was $26,935, what is the new cost, after the increase?
   A. $74,819.44
   B. $36,631.60
   C. $26,971.00
   D. $9,696.60

Let's think about this problem for a minute. If the price has *increased*, is the answer going to be greater than or less than the original price?

Daniel: Greater than.

Ridley: Correct. Therefore, we can eliminate D, since this number is way too low. Now, the increase was only 36%, and choice A is almost three times the original price, so we can eliminate it as well. This leaves only B and C, and C is not much of an increase from the original price, so that leaves B.

An open-ended Number Sense question could look like this:

> 5. Several students have joined together to make a pot of clam chowder for their class. Each student has a recipe that requires different amounts of clams, listed as follows, in pounds.
>
> $2\frac{1}{4}$ $\frac{8}{3}$ $2\frac{1}{8}$ 2.5 $2\frac{1}{3}$
>
> The students want to use the largest number of clams. Which amount should they use?
>
> Explain how you determined which number was largest.

Now, I could go into a nice little discussion of improper fractions, number lines, and common denominators, but you know what? I'm not going to, since that isn't the easiest way to work this problem.

On any open-ended Math question that features fractions *and* decimals, use your calculator to convert all fractions into decimals.

You'll have the technology, so you might as well use it. After changing all the fractions into decimals, you'll notice that 2.66666, or $\frac{8}{3}$, is the largest amount. Write about how you solved it, and there's 2 points!

Key Idea 3: Operations

Daniel: I know all about Operations—it's the wacky doctor's game.

Ridley: Sadly, Daniel, that's not correct—none of these questions will ask you to remove a rubber band called the Charlie Horse. Instead, Operations questions are well-known by another name: *Word Problems.* You will be presented with a situation requiring you to decide whether addition, subtraction, multiplication, or division is needed in order to find the right answer. Since these are word problems, be prepared to do reading. What you'll need to do is to translate the *words* into *math*—either an equation or a diagram. Don't try to work these problems out in your head, as anyone who tries to do that is asking for trouble. Trying to keep track of multiple variables in your head while solving a problem is like juggling with chainsaws—you might be able to get away with it, but if you slip up, the consequences are very painful.

Willy: But doesn't writing everything down take a lot of time?

Ridley: Not really. If you get into the habit of writing everything down as you problem solve, it won't take longer to work out a problem on paper than in your head. Remember, writing everything down eliminates mental errors.

6. Prakash went to an arts show. It cost $4.00 to enter the show. While he was there, Prakash spent money for snacks that cost $1.25 per snack. If Prakash spent $10.25 at the show, which equation could be used to find s, the number of snacks he bought while there?

   A. $1.25s + 4 = 10.25$

   B. $4s + 1.25 + 10.25$

   C. $s = \frac{10.25}{4 + 1.25}$

   D. $s = \frac{10.25}{1.25 + 5}$

> ### Information
>
> On word problems, show your work! Organize the information you are given, labeling any given quantities and identifying exactly what you need to find. Write out the information in the form of an equation or a diagram.

In the problem above, the test makers aren't interested in finding the actual value of s, they just want to see if you know how to find it. This is what I call a "Find the Equation" question. These questions ask you to find the equation which can be used to find the value of a certain variable. In fact, the answer choices all contain the variable in them.

In question 6, we must find the equation that will enable us to find the value of s, so we must translate the words of the question into math. To start, Prakash spent $4.00 to enter the show. Then, he spent $1.25 on each snack. Since he bought s snacks, the amount he spent on the snacks was ($1.25 per snack) $\times$ (s snacks), or $1.25s. So he spent $4.00 to enter the show and $1.25s for the snacks.

The total he spent was $4.00 + $1.25s, or $(4.00 + 1.25s)$. We know he spent a total of $10.25, so the equation for s is $4.00 + 1.25s = 10.25$. This is the same as $1.25s + 4 = 10.25$, which is choice A.

While algebraic formulas were provided in question 6, they won't be on the open-ended questions. For those, you'll have to come up with the proper formula on your own.

7. Charles is making a display case for his collection of autographed baseballs. In order to keep the baseballs separate, he has placed six wooden pegs, each $\frac{2}{3}$ inches wide, in a display case that is $23\frac{3}{5}$ inches long, as shown below. The space at each end of the rack is the same size as the space between any two adjacent pegs in the display case.

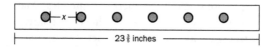

23 ⅗ inches

What is the distance in inches (x) between any two pegs in the display case? Show your work or explain in words how to determine the answer.

Unless you dream about variables (like I sometimes do), it's going to take some work to get this question right. Still, it's solvable if you remain patient and unflustered.

The key here is to set up the proper formula. The entire display case is $23\frac{3}{5}$ inches long, and it is composed only of pegs and spaces. There are 6 pegs $\frac{2}{3}$ inches long and 7 spaces of unknown width x, so our equation looks like:

$$6\left(\frac{2}{3}\right) + 7x = 23\frac{3}{5}$$

Getting the right equation, and explaining why and how, should earn us 1 point right there. Now it's merely a question of doing the math correctly. In the end, $x = 2\frac{4}{5}$ inches, or 2.8 inches.

Operations questions also include ratio problems. With ratio questions, the key is to set up the ratio properly. You'll be provided with one complete ratio and will be asked to complete another ratio.

8. The ratio of students to teachers at Middlebrook High is 7 to 4. If there are 28 teachers at the school, how many students are there?

  A. 16
  B. 28
  C. 49
  D. 196

Daniel: I eliminated B because 28 appears in the question itself. After that, I just guessed C since D seemed too large and A was too small.

X!Frumious: I took the first ratio, $\frac{7}{4}$ and made it equal to the second ratio, $\frac{x}{28}$. Since $\frac{7}{4} = \frac{x}{28}$, the missing number, x, must be 49, answer C.

Key Idea 4: Modeling/Multiple Representation

Ridley: This Key Idea is really geometry. You will be probably be asked one graph question—the whole (x,y) coordinate grid stuff—and a few questions about geometric principles. Make sure you know the definitions for the basic shapes (squares, circles, quadrilaterals, triangles) as well as the geometric concepts such as lines and angles. These formulas and concepts will help you on some problems, but on others, the best technique is something you carry with you at all times: *Your eyes.*

9. A building casts a shadow that is 40 feet long. At the same time Gavin, who is 5 feet tall, casts a shadow 8 feet long. How tall is the building?

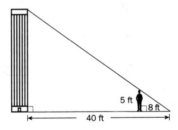

5 ft   8 ft

40 ft

A. 10 feet
B. 12 feet
C. 25 feet
D. 64 feet

You might think you have to do the math for this. If you know the math, that's fine, but since this problem is multiple-choice, there is more than one way to find the answer.

Use your eyes and look at the problem. You will see that the diagram is relatively close to scale. If the shadow is 40 feet long, guess how tall the building might be. Is it about half of the shadow, or more than half?

Willy: I say it's a little more than half.

Ridley: Is it longer than the shadow itself?

Daniel: Definitely not.

Ridley: Well, if it's not longer than the shadow, that means it isn't longer than 40 feet, and we can cross out choice D. Similarly, if you look at the man's height, 5 feet tall, and then look at the building, you should see that A and B are too small. That leaves C, so C it is. Don't worry about the actual math: the real question throughout this test should not be "How do I do the math?" but "How do I answer the question correctly?"

Information

To do the math on question 9, set up a ratio—in this case, $\frac{x}{40} = \frac{5}{8}$.

Using your eyes is the key to solving Geometry questions. However, remember that some questions make it a point of hiding the Geometric concept being tested.

10. A rectangular park is 110 yards long and $43\frac{2}{3}$ yards wide. If a person walked all the way around the outside edge of the park, how many yards would they walk?

   A. $153\frac{2}{3}$ yards

   B. $197\frac{1}{3}$ yards

   C. $263\frac{2}{3}$ yards

   D. $307\frac{1}{3}$ yards

This question asks us to find the perimeter of a rectangle, but the one word that does not appear in the question is . . . *perimeter*! Once you figure out this is a rectangular perimeter question, you need to remember the formula, which is $P = 2\,(\ell + w)$—the Math Reference Sheet doesn't include the formula for perimeter—and plug in the numbers from the question.

Daniel: Ridley, I crossed out A and C, because they both had the fraction $\frac{2}{3}$ in them, and that was the same fraction used in the problem.

Ridley: Good use of elimination, Dan. If you had been unsure about this question, you might have seen the fraction $\frac{2}{3}$ in the problem and incorrectly looked for an answer choice with the same fraction. This

Strategy

Use your eyes to help you eliminate answer choices on geometry questions. Look at the diagram that accompanies the problem to estimate the correct distance with your eyes. Be aware, though, that on diagram questions involving angles, the range of answer choices is usually close together, so using your eyes to eliminate answer choices is not as effective as it is when measuring lines.

isn't *always* true—sometimes the right answer has the same fraction that was in the question—so don't always rule it out, but it's a good guessing technique. Now that you've eliminated A and C, you have a 50/50 chance of getting the right answer even if you don't know how to do the math.

Two more things you should know about the geometry questions concerns three-dimensional objects and congruency. Congruency—which means same size and shape—is a term that is sometimes used on the math test. It is tested in a variety of ways. You'll also need to know the basic three-dimensional shapes, such as cubes, spheres, pyramids, and cones.

The open-ended Geometry questions sometimes look harder than they really are.

11. A telephone pole, which is danger of falling because of rot, stands 75 feet from a swimming pool. The angle of elevation from the swimming pool to the top of the telephone pole is 50°. If the telephone pole falls, determine whether or not it could hit the pool.

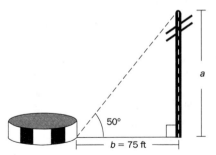

Show your work or explain in words.

Off the top of my head, I can think of three ways to solve this problem.

1. Use my eyes and take a guess.

2. Use the Trigonometric table on the Reference Sheet.

3. Use what I know about triangles.

Angela: I'm leaning toward method 1, but I doubt I'd get full credit if I wrote "the telephone pole could hit the pool because it looks like it could."

Willy: I might use method 2, since the Math Reference sheet is right there, but looking up the tangent of 50° doesn't inspire much confidence in me.

Ridley: Well, Angela might get a point if she guesses correctly, and Willy is probably working the problem the way the test takers want him to, but I'm going for method 3.

You see, we all know that there are 180 degrees in a triangle, right? Well, we have one right angle, which is 90 degrees, and another angle that's 50 degrees. That means the remaining angle is 40 degrees.

Now, the 40 degree angle is opposite the space between the telephone pole and the swimming pool. This is *b*. To find out whether or not the pole could hit the pool, I ask myself, "Is *a* greater than *b*?" If it is, the pole could make a splash. Since the angle opposite *a* is greater than the angle opposite *b*, I think the answer is yes. This is because the larger the angle, the larger the side of the triangle opposite it.

> **Strategy**
>
> At the back of the test, you'll be provided with a ruler and a protractor. Some questions will clearly state that you'll need to use one of these items, but feel free to use them on other questions as well. A ruler can help you to estimate sums on certain problems that provide drawings.

Willy: Using the Trig tables at the front, I got the same answer.

On the Geometry problems, there's often more than one way to solve a question—just be sure you have a good grasp of all the fundamental formulas.

Key Idea 5: Measurement

Ridley: Ladies and gentlemen, start your rulers! Measurement questions ask you to measure various drawings accurately, and also to work with graphs and charts. Chart questions come in two forms: simple and advanced. With simple questions, you'll be asked to *read* the graph correctly. With advanced questions, you'll be asked to *make* a graph.

> **Information**
>
> On the test, you'll be provided with a Mathematics Reference Sheet. It includes a trigonometric table, as well as surface area formulas for a right circular cylinder and a rectangular solid. Don't be intimidated by these complex topics—they're a small part of the test.

As you might expect, the simple chart/graph questions are usually multiple-choice, while the advanced questions are 2- or 3-point open-ended questions. Here's a simple chart question.

12. For one week, a clothing store kept track of the number of customers it had during the week. What is the mean number of customers for that five-day period?

Monday	140
Tuesday	90
Wednesday	250
Thursday	140
Friday	70

   A.   98
   B.   138
   C.   140
   D.   250

Willy: Ridley, what does *mean* mean?

Ridley: To *find the mean* is to find the *average* of a group of numbers. To find the *mean* you add up a group of numbers and then divide that sum by however many numbers there are in the group.

In this simple chart question, you have to read the information and then perform an operation with it (find the average). Add up the number of customers to find the total and then divide that by the number of days, in this case, 5. You get 138, choice B.

Daniel: I got B also, but I used POE. You can cross out C and D because they feature numbers that appeared in the question. Furthermore, if you think about it, D is impossible. I mean, how could the *average* number of customers equal the *highest* number of any day? The average would have to be somewhere between the lowest number of customers and the highest number. That leaves A and B, and if I had to guess, I'd pick B because it's closer to the middle of all those numbers, and isn't that what an average is all about?

Ridley: Here's an example of a more advanced chart/graph question.

13. For one week, a clothing store kept track of the number of customers it had during the week. The table below shows the number of customers for that five-day period.

Monday	140
Tuesday	90
Wednesday	250
Thursday	140
Friday	70

Part A   On the grid below, create a bar graph that shows this information.

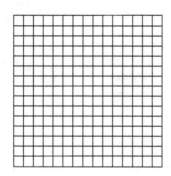

Part B   Complete the circle graph below.

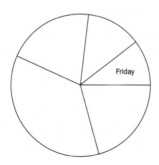

Part C   Determine which graph more clearly
shows that over half of the customers
arrived on either Wednesday or Thursday.
Use the information from both graphs to
justify your answer.

_____

_____

_____

When you create a bar graph, make sure to clearly label the horizontal and vertical axes. Once you get this step, the rest of the graph should fall into place. I recommend putting "Number of Customers" along the vertical axis and "Days" along the horizontal axis, but you can flip those if you want to. Once you have labeled the axes, write in the days of the week along the horizontal axis. As for the vertical axis, what's the greatest number of customers on any day, Willy?

Information

On chart questions that require you to make a bar graph, make sure you clearly label the horizontal and vertical axes.

Willy: There are 250 on Wednesday.

Ridley: Right, so you'll need to go up to at least 250 when you place numbers along the vertical side. How else can you graph the information properly? I recommend units of 25, so each square up on the vertical axis means 25 more customers.

It's also important that you correctly label the circle graph. You need to process the numbers that appear in the chart into sections of the circle graph. Friday is given to you. If you find two sections of the chart that look like they're the exact same size, what days would they be?

Willy: They would be Monday and Thursday, since both those days had 140 customers. And the biggest slice would be Wednesday, since it has the largest number of customers of any day.

Ridley: That leaves only two slices, and since one of them is labeled Friday, the remaining section has to be Tuesday.

Two parts of the question down, one to go. For part C, you might think that a good argument for either the bar or circle graph would get you credit, but you'd be wrong. The correct answer is the circle graph, because it shows the percent of customers on those two days is clearly more than half the circle, and therefore over half the total number of customers. That third point is tough to get, eh? Still, if you labeled the bar graph correctly and filled in the circle graph correctly, you would still get some credit on this question.

In addition to your usual charts and graphs, there may also be a Venn diagram question on the test.

Venn diagram

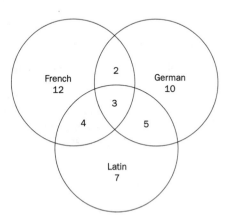

A Venn diagram is a series of interlocking circles designed to visually show information. The previous diagram shows how many students at Mythical Junior High are enrolled in various language classes. The numbers inside the circles show how many students are enrolled in each language, as well as how many students are enrolled in one or more languages. That's the advantage of the Venn diagram. For example, to determine how many students are studying French, you need to add up all the numbers inside the "French" circle.

> O Most Pulchritudinous One, do you remember that Englishman, John Venn, whom we abducted briefly during the mid 20th Century? You know, the one who showed us that cool deal with interlocking circles, and also introduced us to the concept of brunch? That was John Venn.

Daniel: So that would be 12 + 2 + 3 + 4 = 21.

Ridley: Yes. Since those four numbers are all inside the French circle, that's how many students are taking French classes. But each of those numbers—12, 2, 3, and 4—also means something on its own. You see, the number 12 is only inside one circle, the French one, so there are 12 students who are taking French and no other languages. However, the numbers 3 and 4 are also inside the Latin circle, so $3 + 4 = 7$ is the number of students enrolled in both French and Latin classes.

Willy: So $2 + 3 = 5$ is the number of students enrolled in both French and German classes.

Angela: And 3 is the number of students enrolled in all three language classes, since the number 3 is inside all three circles.

Ridley: You're both right. Let's see how you do with a Venn diagram question.

14. Based on the Venn diagram, how many students are enrolled in more than one language class?

A. 3
B. 11
C. 14
D. 29

To find the answer, you need to add up every number that is inside two or more of the circles. So, $4 + 2 + 5 + 3 = 14$, answer C.

Key Idea 6: Uncertainty

Ridley: Although their name does not suggest it, Uncertainty questions certainly fall into two major categories, *estimation* and *probability*. Estimation questions are visual questions that ask you to eyeball a small amount and then decide how many of the small amounts will fit into a bigger amount. An open-ended estimation question might look like this:

15. Carlos is using pebbles to cover the bottom of his goldfish pond. The pebbles come in packages that contain 85 pebbles. Carlos has learned that it takes 38 pebbles to cover the portion of the pond shown in the diagram below.

ESTIMATE the whole number of packages of pebbles that Carlos should purchase to completely cover the bottom of his goldfish pond. Show your work or explain in words how to determine an estimate.

Your first question should be, "How many pebbles do I need in order to cover the bottom of the pond?" Look at the shaded portion and decide how many of those slices are needed to fill the circle.

X!Frumious: Well, if I put two more slices of the same size next to it, I would have one-fourth of the circle. So if it takes 3 slices to cover one-fourth of the circle, I would need 12 slices to cover the whole circle.

Ridley: Correct. Now you have to multiply 38 pebbles (the number needed to fill one slice) by 12. Or, since the question tells you to estimate, you could multiply 40 by 12, and get 480 pebbles.

That alone should earn you 1 point, provided you show your work. To figure out how many packages of pebbles you need, you now have to divide 480 by 85, which is the number of pebbles in each package. If you round 85 off to 80, you get $\frac{480}{80} = 6$. So our answer would be 6 packages—but you would also get credit for an answer of 5 packages, since we have been estimating.

Daniel: Those were two hard-earned points.

Ridley: Let's move on to probability questions. One type of probability question—one that often includes the phrase *how many different*—usually tests whether you can figure out all the possible combinations of a group of items. To help you solve these questions, get into a *multiplying* mindset.

> **Strategy**
>
> *When you see a probability question, get into a multiplying mindset.*

16. Auditions for the jazz band are currently scheduled for 11:00 a.m., 12:00 p.m., 1:00 p.m., 2:00 p.m., and 3:00 p.m. on Monday, Tuesday, Thursday, and Friday of next week. How many different audition choices (consisting of one time and one day) are available?

    A.   5
    B.   16
    C.   20
    D.   25

To find the whole range of choices, you must multiply the different variables together. In this case the variables are the times and the days.

Willy: Since there are five audition times and four days, I would multiply 5×4 to get 20, choice C.

Ridley: Correct. Now, the problems can appear tricky, but once you recognize the *how many different* phrase, things should go smoothly, even if I make the question more difficult, like:

17. Auditions for the jazz band are currently scheduled for 11:00 a.m., 12:00 p.m., 1:00 p.m., 2:00 p.m., and 3:00 p.m. on Monday, Tuesday, Thursday, and Friday of next week, and in rooms 234, 256, and 278. How many audition choices (consisting of one time, one day, and one room) are available?

    A.   80
    B.   60
    C.   20
    D.   9

Ridley: In the modified question, I've added another variable, the three rooms. Still, you solve the questions by multiplying all the variables, in this case $5 \times 4 \times 3$, or five audition times $\times$ four days $\times$ three rooms = 60, choice B.

Key Idea 7: Patterns/Function

Ridley: *Prepare for launch. 6, 5, 4, 3, 2 . . .*

What number comes next? If you can answer that question, you're on the right track for Pattern questions.

18. What number should come next in this pattern?

2, 4, 12, 36, 180, . . .

A. 1,440
B. 1,260
C. 1,080
D. 360

Pattern questions on the 4th Grade New York State Math test are almost always solved by adding or subtracting numbers. However, on the 8th Grade test, these questions are almost always found by *multiplying* numbers (and occasionally, by dividing). So in the problem above, you need to figure out how multiplication is used.

X!Frumious: Well, the first number is multiplied by 2, the second number is multiplied by 3, and the one after that by 4. So I need to multiply 180 by 6 to get . . .

> **Information**
>
> Solutions to pattern problems usually involve multiplication.

Ridley: Answer C! Right!

In an open-ended pattern question, you'll likely be provided with little initial information about the pattern. You must first identify the pattern, and then to be able to use it.

19. Theodore is monitoring the growth of a fast-growing algae. He has discovered that the algae cells reproduce by dividing in half every 40 minutes.

Part A

If Theodore starts out with 2 algae cells, how many cells will there be in 4 hours? Show your work.

Part B

After how many minutes will there be 1,024 algae cells? Show your work.

Daniel: I understand that the pattern is, "multiply by 2 every 40 minutes," but what do I do with that information?

Ridley: Write it down. In question 18, you are provided with the beginning of the pattern, "2, 4, 12, 36, 180." In question 19, you just make a chart like the one below:

0 hr	40 minutes	1 hr, 20 min	2hr	2hr 40 min	3hr, 20 min	4 hr
2	4	8	16	32	64	128

So the answer to Part A is 128, and if we continue to extend the chart, we would reach 1,024 cells at the 6 hour mark.

Willy: So you made a chart to solve a pattern problem. Can you do that?

Ridley: Certainly. Often, you can use the techniques from one question type to help you solve another question type. There's more than one way to skin a cat *and* take the 8th Grade Math test.

And that's all for the Math exam! X!Frumious, check the stopwatch I gave you. What numbers do you see?

Daniel: (*peering over X!Frumious's shoulder*) The watch has been mangled somehow, but it still says, "34 minutes, 8 seconds." Exactly as long as you said it would take.

Ridley: Yippee! Hooray! 2, 4, 6, 8, who do we appreciate?

Everyone: Ridley!

Overview: 8ᵗʰ Grade Math Test Strategies

Strategy 1:   On open ended-questions, plan to spend 4–8 minutes on each.

Strategy 2:   On open ended-questions, make sure to show your work, and give every question your best shot using sound math skills.

Strategy 3:   On all Mathematical Reasoning problems—and throughout the math test on the whole—break up each multi-step question into a series of small steps.

Strategy 4:   On word problems, show your work! Organize the information you are given, labeling any given quantities and identifying exactly what you need to find. Write out the information in the form of an equation or a diagram.

Strategy 5:   Use your eyes to help you eliminate answer choices on geometry questions. Look at the diagram that accompanies the problem to estimate the distance.

Strategy 6:   Using your eyes can help you eliminate wrong answers when examining diagram questions that involve **lines**. But don't rely on your eyes for diagram questions that involve **angles**. The range of answer choices for angle questions is usually close together, so you won't be able to eliminate answer choices just by looking at them.

Strategy 7:   On chart questions that require you to make a bar graph, make sure you clearly label the horizontal and vertical axes.

Strategy 8:   When you see a probability question, get into a multiplying mindset.

Sample Questions—Mathematics

1. What volume of water can be kept in an aquarium that is 30 feet long, 22 feet wide, and 8 feet deep?

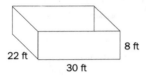

A. 416 cubic feet
B. 660 cubic feet
C. 5,280 cubic feet
D. 15,840 cubic feet

2. The city traffic department set up a system to count the number of cars that passed through the Ash and Main intersection from Monday through Friday. What was the mean (average) number of cars per day for the five-day period?

Day	Number of Cars
Monday	160
Tuesday	160
Wednesday	140
Thursday	220
Friday	240

A. 140
B. 160
C. 184
D. 240

3. On a digital scale, a peach weighs 0.364 pounds. What is the weight of the peach rounded to the nearest hundredth of a pound?

A. 0.004
B. 0.36
C. 0.367
D. 0.4

4. While at the school store, Markus can choose from the items listed below. How many different choices consisting of 1 pen, 1 notebook, and 1 pencil does he have?

Pens	Notebooks	Pencils
Blue	spiral	plastic
Red	plain	wood
Black		mechanical

A. 3
B. 6
C. 8
D. 18

5. In the figure below, what is the degree measure of angle q?

A. 150
B. 80
C. 70
D. 40

6. What number should come next in this pattern?

1, 2, 2, 4, 8, 32, ...

A. 16
B. 64
C. 126
D. 256

7. A swimming pool has a filter that processes 6 quarts of water per minute. How many **gallons** of water does the filter process every **hour**?

A. 30 gal
B. 60 gal
C. 90 gal
D. 360 gal

8. Michelle bought a hat on sale at 80% off the regular price of $42. A way to find the amount of money Michelle saved is to multiply $42 by

   A. $\frac{4}{5}$

   B. $\frac{21}{40}$

   C. $\frac{1}{5}$

   D. $\frac{2}{25}$

9. The picture below shows the shadow cast by a tree.

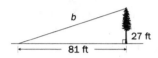

   How long is the line segment *b*?

   A. between 70 and 80 feet
   B. between 80 and 90 feet
   C. between 90 and 100 feet
   D. between 100 and 110 feet

10. By the shortest route, what is the highway mileage between Elgin and Blanco?

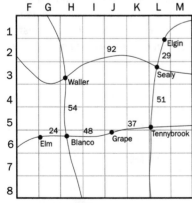

   A. 117 miles
   B. 128 miles
   C. 136 miles
   D. 165 miles

11. The graph below shows the geographic breakdown of the students of Strack High.

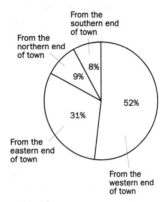

   Which conclusion can be drawn from the data shown on the graph?

   A. Less than half of all students are from the western end of town.
   B. More than one-third of all students are from the eastern end of town.
   C. Most students are from the eastern or northern part of town.
   D. There are more students from the northern part of town than there are from the southern part of town.

12. According to a recent poll, 43% of the employees at Mike's Gym went to college and received a degree in physical therapy. If there are 89 employees at Mike's Gym, what is the best estimate of the number of employees who are physical therapy graduates?

   A. 10
   B. 20
   C. 40
   D. 50

13. In Mr. Fischer's homeroom class, 17 out of 32 students are right-handed. Which proportion could be used to determine r, where $r\%$ is the percentage of students who are right-handed?

    A. $\frac{17}{32} = \frac{r}{100}$

    B. $\frac{32}{r} = \frac{100}{17}$

    C. $\frac{32}{17} = \frac{r}{100}$

    D. $\frac{r}{32} = \frac{17}{100}$

14. A basic cable television package costs $36.50 per month. Each additional channel costs $3.50. Lynn's cable bill costs $61 per month. If c represents the number of additional cable channels Lynn has, which equation could be used to find c?

    A. $(36.50 + 3.50)c = 61$
    B. $61 = 36.50c + 3.50$
    C. $36.50 - 3.50c = 61$
    D. $36.50 + 3.50c = 61$

15. A grocer has discovered that roughly 1 out of every 7 bushels of lettuce she receives contains a rotten plant. If the grocer receives a shipment of 60 bushels of lettuce, which is a reasonable number of bushels with rotten plants to expect?

    A. Less than 7
    B. Between 8 and 9
    C. Between 9 and 11
    D. Between 11 and 13

16. A post oak is 93 feet tall. If it grows 1.5 feet per year, how many years will it take until the tree reaches 120 feet?

    A. Just under 2 years
    B. 9 years
    C. 18 years
    D. 27 years

17. If 1 marble is selected at random from a bag containing 6 blue marbles, 12 red marbles, 18 green marbles, and 24 black marbles, what is the probability that the marble will be green?

    A. $\frac{1}{12}$

    B. $\frac{1}{6}$

    C. $\frac{3}{10}$

    D. $\frac{1}{3}$

18. Monti has to place a length of rope around the outer edge of a well so that no one accidentally falls in. If the well has a diameter of 14 feet, which is the shortest length of rope that will completely encircle the well?

    (Use $\pi = \frac{22}{7}$)

    A. 44 feet
    B. 33 feet
    C. 22 feet
    D. 14 feet

19. A recipe for a pot of gumbo calls for $\frac{4}{5}$ cup of okra to make 8 bowls of gumbo. How many cups of okra would be needed to make 10 pots of gumbo?

    A. $\frac{4}{5}$ cup

    B. 8 cups

    C. 10 cups

    D. $12\frac{1}{2}$ cups

20. A chef wants to make $\frac{2}{3}$ of a recipe for wild rice. The recipe calls for 16 pounds of wild rice. How many pounds will the chef need altogether?

    A. 8 pounds

    B. $10\frac{2}{3}$ pounds

    C. $11\frac{1}{3}$ pounds

    D. 24 pounds

21. A soft-drink company did a survey to see how many people had drunk their two soft drinks, Jooky and Cajon Lite. The results are shown below.

    R = Set of 400 people surveyed
    J = Set of people who drank Jooky
    C = Set of adults who drank Cajon Lite

    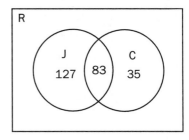

    How many people surveyed had not drunk either soft drink?

    A. 83
    B. 155
    C. 238
    D. 245

22. Mr. Grubeck's class has been collecting data of rainfall in New York. The table below shows the amount of rain for seven New York cities in August 2001.

City	Total Rainfall (in centimeters)	Departure from Normal (in centimeters)
Buffalo	14.9	− 5.8
Ithaca	28.6	+ 12.6
Niagara Falls	35.9	+ 18.4
Ossining	8.4	− 0.5
Schenectady	16.5	− 0.2
Utica	17.5	+ 4.8
Watertown	2.1	− 2.0

Part A

What was the mean rainfall for all of these cities in August 2001? Show your work.

Part B

Using the information in the table above, calculate the normal August rainfall, in centimeters, for Utica.

Part C

In terms of average rainfall, was August 2001 a wetter or a drier month for these combined cities? Show your work

23. Shade in $\frac{3}{8}$ of the rectangle below.

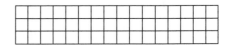

What percent of the rectangle is shaded? Show your work.

24. In the expression below, insert two sets of parentheses so that the expression is equal to 12.

$$\frac{4 \times 15 + 2^2 - 4}{3 - 2 \times 6}$$

Now show the steps you used to simplify the expression to show that it equals 12. Show your work.

English Language Arts

Session Leader: Angela Lupino

> O Most Truculent Czar of the Galaxy, this meeting took place at Angela's room. There were books everywhere! Many were on bookshelves, but others were stacked up from the floor to create teetering, six-foot columns of books. At first, I was sure that I was mere moments away from being brained by the Time Life Series: *Gunfighters of the Wild West* set of books balanced unsteadily near my head, looming like some leather-bound jungle animal in eight easy-to-read volumes. Luckily, no such disaster occurred.
>
> —X!Frumious

NAME: Angela Ines Lupino

BORN: November 27, 1989
Sagua la Grande, Cuba

NOTES: Angela showed a remarkable ability to read and comprehend at an early stage of life. She finished all the Curious George books by age four, read 10 books of Charles Dickens by age 11, and wrote her first book at age 12, though she has yet to find a publisher willing to print an autobiography of someone who can't even drive. She was voted by classmates as "Most Likely to Write a Thousand-Page Novel While in High School."

Angela: Greetings, everyone, and welcome to my humble room and library. I hope you're all comfortable.

Daniel: There are books everywhere!

Willy: Where's the floor? I can't see it. Well, not a lot of it, anyway.

Angela: Trust me, Willy, it's there. What else could the books on my floor be resting on? I know many people think I read too much, although I can tell you right now that such a thing is impossible. There are simply too many good books out there, and no one person could read them all. Speaking of reading, let's talk about the 8th Grade English Language Arts (ELA) test, shall we?

The ELA test assesses how well you are able to read a variety of materials, listen closely, and respond in writing. You will read literary and informational passages, and answer multiple-choice and essay questions based on what you have read. You will also listen to an informational passage, respond to short answer questions, and write an essay demonstrating your listening comprehension.

Overview: NYS 8th Grade English Language Arts test

Session 1	**Part 1**	Read 4 passages and answer 25 multiple-choice questions
	Part 2	Listen to a passage and write 3 short responses and 1 extended response
Session 2	**Part 1**	Read 2 related passages and write 3 short responses and 1 extended response
	Part 2	Write a composition
Time		90 minutes for each session
Scoring		You will receive an overall score of 1 (deficient) through 4 (advanced). Your receive credit only for those questions that you answer correctly. There is no penalty for wrong answers, and an answer left blank receives no credit.

This exam lasts two days and has a variety of formats. According to the New York State Education Department, there are three main ideas, or Learning Standards, that we're tested on. They are:

New York State Learning Standards

1. **Information and Understanding:** *Students collect data, facts, and ideas; discover relationships, concepts, and generalizations; acquire and interpret information.* In other words, you will read a sentence like "The quick brown fox jumped over the lazy dog" and be able to understand what it means well enough to answer questions like "What color is the fox?" or "Does the dog appear to have a job?"

2. **Literary Response and Expression:** *Students will read and listen to texts and relate these texts to their own lives; they will develop an understanding of the diverse social, historical, and cultural dimensions of the work; and they will be able to write down their own thoughts and ideas in proper English.* To paraphrase, you'll read a sentence like "The quick brown fox jumped over the lazy dog" and be able to write an essay "describing any experiences you might have had with a quick brown fox and what you learned from it" or write several paragraphs wherein you describe "some possible reasons that the dog is so lazy, and what could be done to change it."

3. **Critical Analysis and Evaluation:** *As listeners and readers, students will analyze experiences, ideas, information, and issues presented by others; they will use proper English and be able to convey their own opinions and judgments on experiences, ideas, information, and issues.* Translation: you will be able to write an essay like "Why a certain brown fox needs to slow down before someone gets hurt."

Not every session section covers all three Learning Standards. Session 1, Part 1, addresses Learning Standards 1 and 2. This first part of the test emphasizes our ability to understand and answer questions about what we read. The second part of the test switches to Standards 2 and 3, where a considerable amount of writing is required. Here, you'll have to get into the mood to say what is on your mind, or it will be a long test.

Although this might sound simple, it's not. Some of us have had little experience with literary interpretation, and even if we have, we might have a hard time expressing our ideas eloquently under test conditions. Nevertheless, that's what you'll need to do to get a good score on each section after the initial multiple-choice section.

Information

Think of the 8th Grade test as four different tests:

Test 1: *multiple-choice questions*

Test 2: *listening and open-ended questions*

Test 3: *reading and open-ended questions*

Test 4: *a written composition*

Daniel: It sounds like we should think of the test as four different tests. The first test is multiple-choice questions; the second test is listening and answering open-ended questions; the third test is reading and answering open-ended questions; and the fourth test is writing an essay.

Angela: For most of us, Session 1 will be the easier of the two sessions, because reading a passage and answering multiple-choice questions is probably something we've done before. In Session 2, we'll read longer, more involved passages, and answer short and extended responses for each. Then, we'll write an essay.

Now let's talk about the passages themselves. The reading passages will average about 800 words each and can be broken down into three main categories:

1. Literary passages

2. Informational passages

3. Oddball passages

As you might guess, the literary and informational passages are exactly what their names suggest. A literary (or fiction) passage usually tells a story, often about someone our age, and often has an uplifting or inspiring theme. An informational (or nonfiction) passage is typically educational or instructional, perhaps in the form of a biography or a recollection of a famous event.

The third type of passage is what I call the Oddball passage, since it comes in a variety of different styles: it might be a letter of recommendation, a poster from a play, or even a page from an instruction manual. Despite its unique format, an Oddball passage should be treated in the same way as are the other passage types.

> **Strategy**
>
> *Don't let unusual reading passages bother you. Except for their different format, Oddball passages are just like fiction and nonfiction passages.*

Now, as far as *how* to work through the reading passages, work through them in whatever order you are comfortable with.

The fact that you're going to answer every question doesn't mean you have to start with question 1 and end with question 25. Many of you have taken a reading test of some kind before, so you might know if you prefer literary over informational passages. If you enjoy fiction passages, answer the questions to those passages first, and then move on to the nonfiction passages. Of course, you have to make sure to fill in the proper ovals, since you will be out of sequence, but that shouldn't be hard to do.

Daniel: Do I have to follow the order of the passages?

Angela: Not at all. You can use the number of questions per passage to determine which passages to work first. For instance, if you have the choice between starting with a shorter passage with 9 questions or a longer passage with 4 questions, you might want to work on the shorter passage first because it will take less time to read and it includes more questions. Remember, the goal on the ELA test is to answer questions, not read passages, so focus first on the passages that have the most questions. Of course, you'll have to work the longer passages eventually, but since you're fresher at the start of the test, use that time to your advantage.

Strategy

Take control of the test.

- Work through the problems in whatever order YOU are most comfortable with.

- If you do answer the questions out of sequence, make sure you remember to fill in the proper ovals.

- Try focusing first on the passages that have the most questions. Since you are fresher at the start of the test, it is a good idea to get more questions out of the way.

Here's a chart which has my pacing suggestions for the test:

For This Activity . . .	Spend This Much Time
Reading a passage	5–7 minutes per passage
Multiple-choice questions	1–2 minutes per question
0–2 point short responses	about 5 minutes per question
0–3 point extended responses	10–15 minutes per question

Daniel: I'm not a fast reader. Can I take more time to read a passage?

Angela: Since this is a timed test, and all the time you spend reading the passage takes away from the time you have to answer questions, I wouldn't recommend it. You want to read the passage to get a general idea of what is going on, and then start answering questions. In most of our regular school classes, we learn about a topic and then take a test to see how well we remember what we have learned. This isn't the best way to approach this section of the test, however.

The key to succeeding on this test is to realize that you can work through the problems any way you like. By doing this, you should gain some confidence in your ability to answer any question correctly.

Before I discuss each question type, let me provide you with a sample reading passage typical of what you'll see on the test.

The Beautiful Summer Day

"Hey, Margaret, why don't you come play softball with us?" asked Margaret's brother Juan. "It's a beautiful day outside." Juan was standing in the doorway holding his bat and two gloves. Behind him his friends Ashok and Joey were waiting on the front steps of the house.

Outside the day was bright and sunny, one of the best days in what had been a very hot summer. Yet even though the beautiful day was tempting, Margaret did not feel like going outside. "Thanks, Juan, but I am just not in the mood to play softball right now. You go on."

"Okay, sister, but school's starting soon, and we won't get many more chances to play softball on a Wednesday afternoon. My friends and I will be at Grompton Park if you want to catch up." Juan picked up a baseball cap and left the house.

Margaret watched her younger brother leave and then let out a deep sigh. Juan was right. School was starting soon, and she should be spending the time before her senior year started to enjoy herself and have some fun. Unfortunately, Margaret was worried about the upcoming year too much to enjoy herself. In some ways, she was excited about the prospect of applying to college, but at the same time it frightened her. What if she did not get into the college of her choice, or any college at all? Margaret hoped to be a music major in college. She knew she was a very good violinist, but music schools were very competitive, and some of them were also fairly expensive. Margaret's parents would help her out financially as much as they could, but Margaret knew she would have to come up with a portion of the money herself. She had worked at her father's office for the first part of the summer, and had earned a little money that way, but the project she had been working on was finished. Margaret knew she would have to find a job during the school year, and although she had worked and gone to school before, it did not leave her with as much free time as she would like.

Margaret went to her room and read for about thirty minutes, but even a book by her favorite author could not help her mood. She went into the study to see if her mother was working on her latest painting, but she was not there. However, there was a slip of paper left on the table addressed to her. Margaret picked up the note and read it:

Dear Margaret,

Someone named Teresa called for you this morning while you were in the shower. She asked you to give her a call at 555-8645. I had to go out and buy some more art supplies, but I should be home by 4:30.

The note was a little puzzling to Margaret at first. She had one friend named Teresa, but she lived in Buffalo, which was over 200 miles away. But since the number Mom wrote down was a local number, that must mean that Teresa was in town. Margaret and Teresa had met during band summer camp two years ago, and quickly became good friends. Teresa was an excellent flute player, and the two of them had even played together on several occasions. Still, Margaret did not go to band summer camp this year, and she had not heard from Teresa in several months.

Margaret dialed the number her Mom had left her. After several rings, a male voice answered, "Hello?"

"Hello, this is Margaret Brantley. May I speak to Teresa?"

"Sure, let me just find her," the man replied. "I think she's in the kitchen with her brother." The line went silent for a while, and then Teresa's voice said, "Margaret? Is that you?"

"It certainly is," she replied. "How are you, Teresa?"

"I'm wonderful!" exclaimed Teresa. "My parents just moved to town, so now I live only a few miles away."

"That's great, Teresa!"

"And there's more," continued Teresa. "My father got the job as the head chef at Bertram's, and they're looking for a group of musicians to play there on the weekends. I asked if I could get the job, and the owner of Bertram's agreed, but only if I could find a quartet. I have a cello player, and a clarinetist, but we need a violinist. Are you interested? It pays very well."

Margaret did not hesitate at all. "You bet I am! What do I need to do?"

Teresa told her. "Our first practice is tomorrow at 10:00. Can you make it?" Margaret told her she could, and Teresa gave Margaret her new address. Then she ended the conversation, claiming that she had to help unpack.

Margaret put the phone down in an exuberant mood. For such a short phone call, it contained a lot of good news. Margaret looked down at her feet and noticed her softball glove lying underneath the kitchen table. She picked it up and headed out the door for Grompton Park. After all, she thought, it would be a shame to waste such a beautiful day.

Multiple-Choice Questions

Angela: There are four types of multiple-choice questions on this section:

- Word Meaning Questions

- Supporting Idea Questions

- Summarization Questions

- Inference and Generalization Questions

If you were to approach this multiple-choice portion like a normal school test, you would read a passage, try to memorize its content, and answer the questions. But doing that here is a waste of time. Instead, read the passage first to understand the main point and get a good idea of what the facts are—and where they're located. Then, answer the questions, but refer back to the passage to make sure your answers are correct.

Ridley: What if I look back at the passage but can't find the answer to a question?

Angela: Then you would use POE to eliminate some answer choices, take an educated guess, and move on. In general, you only need to get about 70% of the questions correct to pass, so there's no need to panic about—or spend ten minutes on—any one question.

Word Meaning Questions

Angela: Word Meaning questions test your vocabulary knowledge. There won't be many of these on the test, but the strategy used to attack them is useful for the entire test, so listen closely.

A reading passage will contain a difficult word, like *exuberant*. The passage will be followed by a Word Meaning question that looks like this:

In the passage, the word *exuberant* means—

There are two ways to answer this question: either you know what it means, or you figure out what it means by looking at the words and sentences around it. I recommend the second method, which is to read around the word, and take an educated guess about what it means. That's also called reading in *context*.

X!Frumious: That sounds hard.

Angela: It's easy once you get the hang of it. All of you have learned words in context. Take the sentence, "Maria feigned being sick so she could stay home from school." If you don't know what *feigned* means, you can still figure it out by looking at the rest of the sentence. It means *faked*.

Strategy

There are two ways to get the correct answer on a Word Meaning question:

1. know the meaning already; or

2. figure out what the word means by looking at how it fits into the rest of the sentence and phrase.

Here's another example. Suppose we heard a phone ringing and I said, "Could you please pick up that mackinute? I'm expecting an important call." What do I mean by *mackinute*?

Daniel: I believe you intend for it to mean a *telephone*.

Angela: Exactly! You figured out the word by using the clue words like *pick up* and *important call* to deduce the word's meaning. Try the problem below, referring back to *The Beautiful Summer Day* passage.

1. In the passage, the word *exuberant* means—

    A. spirited
    B. fretful
    C. disillusioned
    D. capable

Look at the sentence after *exuberant*, and determine what kind of word *exuberant* could be. Is it a positive or negative type of word?

Ridley: I would assume it stands for something positive, since Margaret just received all that good news.

Angela: Right. And if we know that *exuberant* is a positive word, we can use POE to rule out choices B and C, both negative words. That leaves A or D, and since Margaret seems happier than efficient, A is the correct choice.

If you like answering Word Meaning questions, here's something you can do during the test. Before reading a passage for the first time, look to see if a Word Meaning question follows the passage. If there is one, figure out what the word means as soon as you read it, and then go straight to the question to answer it.

Daniel: Yeah, why not? I know the word is going to show up as a question, so why not answer it as soon as I see it?

Ridley: Oh, I don't think that's a good idea for me. I prefer reading the entire passage to get the general idea, and then going to the questions. I'm afraid I'd lose my train of thought if I left the passage midway to go answer a question.

Angela: The choice is yours. Do whatever you are most comfortable with. Of course, Ridley, when you get to the Word Meaning question, go directly to where it appears in the passage and reread the sentences around it. I recommend starting two sentences before the word, and reading through until two sentences after it, just to make sure you understand the context.

Learning how to answer Word Meaning questions will actually help you approach the entire reading test because it trains you to refer to the passage to find the correct answer.

Also, a question might ask for the meaning of an entire phrase or sentence, like "What did Margaret mean when she said, 'it would be a shame to waste such a beautiful day' at the end of the story?" You would answer this the same way you would approach any Word Meaning question—read the sentences around the phrase in question and determine its meaning from the context of the story.

> **Strategy**
>
> When you come across a new word for the first time, you might want to figure out what it means right away and go straight to the Word Meaning question to answer it.

Supporting Idea Questions

Angela: Supporting Idea questions focus on small facts stated within a reading passage—facts that you would probably not remember correctly if you read the passage just once and went on to the questions. Answers to these questions are always directly stated in the passage, so make sure you refer to the text as needed. Here's an example:

O Galactic Uberdude, at first I was puzzled by this story, but then I learned that, unlike us, humans do not usually wear ducks as headgear. (Truly, these humans have no sense of fashion.) I also learned the hard way that Earth ducks are not the well-spoken intellectual philosophers that our Kronhorstian ducks are. However, both duck breeds eat bread crumbs when you throw them some.

A man in a blue business suit walks into a bank wearing a large green duck on his head. The bank teller looks at him and asks, "Is it hard to keep that thing balanced like that?"

"Not really," replied the duck. "I've got sticky, webbed feet."

Supporting Idea questions related to the story above might be, "What color was the man's suit?" or "What size was the duck?"

The main pitfall in Supporting Idea questions is when you *sort of* remember the answer, and an answer choice looks right, so you pick it. But it's wrong! Don't try to answer these questions from memory; it will only hurt your score. Going back to *The Beautiful Summer Day* passage:

2. In the story, Margaret's mother was not around because she—

   A. went to buy art supplies
   B. was in the shower
   C. was at Grompton Park
   D. went to play softball

This isn't a central fact in the story, but it is mentioned, and the key is to find where in the passage it is. This is why, when reading the passage for the first time, you should try to get a general idea of *what* events occur *when*. If you do that well, you'll head straight to the note that says Mom went to buy art supplies, and you'll see choice A is correct.

Ridley: Are there any good elimination techniques to use on this question?

Angela: Not as many as for other questions, because on the one hand, the answer is taken directly from the passage—you either find it or you don't. On the other hand, if you read that Juan is at Grompton Park and he's playing softball, you could correctly assume that C and D are incorrect answer choices put there to trap any student who confuses Juan's actions with his mother's activities. But even if you cross out C and D, it's still in your best interest to look for the precise answer, because it will be there somewhere.

Summarization Questions

Angela: I started this study group by saying you should first read a passage to figure out the main idea or topic. Not only will this help you understand the passage better, it will also help you to answer Summarization questions. Most of these questions will simply ask "What is the main idea of this passage?" or "What is the best summary of this passage?" To answer them, figure out the main point or topic of each passage. When looking over the answer choices for a *literary* passage, look for the answer choice that is positive-sounding and broad in scope. When looking over the answer choices for an *informational* passage, think about the author's purpose in writing the passage.

When figuring out the big picture of a passage, it helps to understand the people who wrote the passage in the first place. The people who write these reading passages are educational writers who try to write positive, character-building stories for eighth graders. With this in mind, you'll never see reading passages that discuss gambling addiction or teenagers dying overseas in a senseless foreign war. Instead, the test includes uplifting biographies of inspirational people as well as stories about students our age who overcome obstacles and become better people for it. So when you answer the question, pay close attention to the most positive-sounding, and the most uplifting answer choice available, as it will be a good choice for the correct answer. To demonstrate, let's look at a question from a literary passage none of us have even seen.

> **Strategy**
>
> To answer a Summarization question, read the passage and state the main idea or topic in your own words. Look for the answer choice that captures that main idea or topic. Watch out for answer choices that may be small details in the passage—you may have read about them, and they may indeed be true—but they're not summary statements.

3. What is the best summary of this passage?

   A. Joy and her mother use a wooden cage baited with chicken to catch a large opossum.
   B. Despite the difficulties presented by Morris, Joy and her mother decide to still pick berries in the nearby field.
   C. Joy believes the large and cunning Morris may be the same opossum that Joy's mother once tried to catch.
   D. Although their efforts to catch the opossum fail, Joy develops a deep respect for the animal and gains more respect for her mother's spirit and endurance.

We know nothing about this passage, but we do know about the writers of the test, so here's how to answer this question. The passage seems to be a literary passage (fiction), since it looks like a story about a girl and her mother. Choice A might be a fact from the passage, but it's not very positive nor does it seem to be a main idea, so we can eliminate it. Choice A might be a good selection if this was a Supporting Idea question. B could be the main idea, and C is the same as A—it might be a fact from the passage, but there's nothing very positive about it. D, however, has a warm, uplifting ending that communicates a thoughtful conclusion of what has happened in the passage. It's the correct response.

Daniel: That's all there is to it?

Angela: Yes. Hopefully, Daniel, you already had an idea that the main idea of the passage had something to do with Joy and her mom sharing a bonding experience, which would make D all the more obvious choice. The key to identifying the main idea is to read the passage and state in your own words what the passage is about. However, even without that, we guessed and answered the question correctly.

Now let's try a question from *The Beautiful Summer Day* passage.

4. What is the best summary of this passage?

   A. Margaret's chances of attending college improve after she receives a job offer, leading her to regain her optimism about the future.
   B. Margaret's ability as a musician leads a local restaurant manager to ask her to play at the restaurant.
   C. Margaret knows she will have to do well in school in order to succeed in her goal of going to college.
   D. Worried about having a lack of funds, Margaret initially turns down her brother's offer to play softball at the park.

X!Frumious: Well, B is not even accurate, so it should go. C and D are both true, but there's nothing really broad or positive about either one, so I picked Choice A, which is uplifting. Also, I felt that the point of the passage was something like, "Margaret starts out bumming that she doesn't have a job, but then gets in a good mood because her friend lands her one." Choice A is a good paraphrase of that idea.

Angela: Correct! In addition to the questions that ask for the main idea or summary of the whole passage, there may also be some questions that ask about the main idea of a smaller chunk of a passage—one or two specific paragraphs. Solve these questions the same way you solve other Summarization questions; identify the main point of that paragraph, and look for the positive answer choice.

Inference and Generalization Questions

Angela: Inference and Generalization questions ask you to draw a conclusion based on information you have read—in other words, to infer an answer from what is contained in the passage. You won't find the answers to these questions directly in the passage, but you'll still want to examine the text for important information. Just don't expect the answer to be obvious.

Supporting Idea question:

5. In the story, Margaret's mother was not around because she—

   A. went to buy art supplies
   B. was in the shower
   C. was at Grompton Park
   D. went to play softball

Inference question on the same topic:

6. When Margaret's mother left the house, the place that she will most likely visit is—

   A. Grompton Park
   B. Teresa's house
   C. Bertram's Restaurant
   D. a painting and crafts store

Since Inference questions don't ask for information directly spelled out in the passage, they often contain words and phrases like *most likely*, *probably*, *might*, or *suggests*. In question 6 above, there's no way to know where Margaret's mother will go, so the question must contain the phrase *will most likely*.

Strategy

Inference questions ask you to draw conclusions based on information you have read. Look for clues in the exact wording of the question to help you find the answer. Remember, the answer won't be spelled out in the text.

Think of these questions as two-step questions. First, find the clue, and then, apply it to the answer choices to find the right response. In *The Beautiful Summer Day* passage, Margaret's mom doesn't say exactly where she is going, but she leaves to go buy art supplies. If we know she needs art supplies (Step 1), (Step 2) would be to pick the appropriate answer choice.

Daniel: That would be D, since you can most likely buy art supplies at a painting and crafts store.

Angela: Correct. These questions might take a little more effort, but they're not necessarily harder than other question types. In fact, you can still use POE on them. Just keep in mind that the writers of the literature (fiction) passages often lean toward the positive, uplifting side. Here's another question.

7. The author of this passage suggests that the writings and accomplishments of W. E. B. Du Bois will probably be—

   A. awarded national honors.
   B. not very useful to future scholars of African American history.
   C. meaningful to future generations.
   D. disregarded by modern human rights organizations.

Daniel: I'd get rid of B and D, since they are both negative.

Angela: That leaves A and C, and from there it's a 50/50 guess unless you look back at the passage. Of course, since there is no passage, I would pick C, since this answer is more vague and therefore harder to disprove.

The 8th Grade ELA test ends up being a pretty involved test, since it has a lot of time-consuming Inference questions that make you search for clues, or evidence, that will help you answer the questions. It would be a much simpler test if all the questions were Supporting Idea questions, but that's not the case. Since most of the questions are Inference problems, you have to use the two-step process. Take the example below, from *The Beautiful Summer Day* passage.

> 8. The author of this passage gives you reason to believe that Margaret—
>
>   A. enjoys playing the violin.
>   B. has many friends her own age.
>   C. is still working for her father.
>   D. plays softball with her brother every week.

Sometimes on a question like this, it's easier to find all the incorrect answers instead of the one correct answer. That means we'll have to look at the passage to check these answers. We know that Teresa is Margaret's friend, but that doesn't mean she has many friends, so B is out. And while Juan asks Margaret to play softball once, nothing states that this is a weekly occurrence, so D is out. C is wrong because the passage states that Margaret is no longer working at Pop's office. That leaves A, which I'll pick.

> O Nictitating One, there are numerous parts of the passage that suggest that Margaret enjoys playing the violin. There's the fact she wants to be a music major, and her readiness to play violin with Teresa at the restaurant.

Occasionally an Inference question will ask you to determine the emotional state of the author or one of the characters. These questions look like the one below, which is from *The Beautiful Summer Day* passage.

> 9. In the first paragraph, the author establishes a mood of—
>
>   A. anxiety
>   B. remorse
>   C. anger
>   D. anticipation

If this question was referring to a literary passage (fiction), the answer would likely be a positive-sounding answer choice, which means B and C are unlikely to be correct. The reason for this is simple. The writers of these reading passages try to communicate positive, uplifting themes, and so there's little room for characters who are vicious, hateful, or irrational. So if you had a question with the following answer choices, picking choice D is a safe bet.

A. vicious
B. hateful
C. irrational
D. agreeable

Even though this is the pattern, it still helps to check your work with the passage. Consider the Margaret passage. Is she in a good mood when the story begins?

Ridley: Not really.

Angela: Exactly. So if this question asked you to describe Margaret's mood at the beginning of the story, you would not be looking for a positive answer. Because of this, if we look at question 9, the answer is A, since Margaret is anxious about her future. So it pays to check with the passage, but just bear in mind that most of the time the warm, fuzzy choice is correct.

Information

On questions that ask you about the author or character's emotional state, look for the positive-sounding answer choice. Most of the time, that will be the correct answer, but to be sure that your selection is correct, check your answer choice with the information in the passage.

Listening and Open-Ended Questions

Angela: After you complete the multiple-choice section, you'll come to the listening comprehension section. Make sure you're comfortable with taking off your multiple-choice hat and replacing it with your writing cap. You won't be able to write just anything—you'll have to really address the task at hand.

Here's what will happen: A teacher will read a passage aloud twice. You'll then be required to answer several open-ended questions about the reading—3 short-response and 1 extended-response. Among other things, you may be asked to draw conclusions, to compare or contrast, to explain certain relationships, or to identify the main idea.

For This Listening Activity . . .	Spend This Amount of Time
Listening and note taking	5–15 minutes total
3 short-answer questions	5–8 minutes each
1 extended-response question	5 minutes planning, 10–15 minutes writing and any remaining time proofreading

The passage will be preceded by a short introduction. You'll be allowed to take notes throughout the reading on one page in the test. Use these notes to help you answer the questions.

This section is meant to examine your listening comprehension. In order to get the most from these readings, you'll need to approach them strategically—you won't have time to write down every detail or idea. Therefore, plan to take notes in the following way.

First, before your teacher begins to read the passage aloud, draw a note-taking chart in the appropriate space in your test booklet. Divide the chart into two sections. In one section, you'll record the main characters and the basic message of the story. In the other section, you'll list important details that complete the story.

The passage will be read twice. The first time through, listen for just the main idea. As you listen, take some notes about the main characters and the main idea, but don't get caught up writing down lots of things or focusing on details. At this point, you want to make sure you're comfortable with what the whole story means. Since you'll be asked

Strategy

In the listening comprehension section, you'll be expected to draw conclusions and explain relationships about the story you have heard. To do this well, you'll want to take good notes as you listen. The best way to take notes is to:

- Draw a note-taking chart in the appropriate space in your test booklet;

- Divide the chart into two sections;

- In one section, record the main characters and the basic message of the story;

- In the other section, list important details that complete the story.

to draw conclusions, make inferences, and explain relationships, you can't afford to be distracted by details. Then, for the second reading, listen closely for details and fill in your chart more completely.

Daniel: Why don't I just start taking notes right off the bat, and write down as much as possible?

Angela: Well, if you're an expert at shorthand, you can do that, and you could treat this section like the previous reading passage section. However, since most of us aren't shorthand experts, writing down everything you hear isn't the best approach, mainly because you write down a lot of worthless material while sacrificing the understanding of the story. By listening closely to the passage the first time, you get an idea of *what* the passage is about, and what events occur *when*.

By learning the main idea, when you hear the story for the second time you can write down key supporting facts. For instance, suppose your teacher chose to read *The Beautiful Summer Day* aloud for this section. What would your notes look like? Here are some sample notes:

> **Strategy**
>
> Sometimes the listening passage will be accompanied by some words and definitions that you'll need to know as you listen. Be sure to look over these words early on so that you can get a sense of what they mean before the passage is read.

Key Characters	Details
Margaret	Can't find job,
Teresa	college pricey.
Juan (maybe)	
	Gets call from friend,
Main Idea	moved to town. Friend
	lines up music gig.
Marg worried about	
senior year—wants	Problem solved for
to be music major.	Marg.
	Marg changes
	attitude, goes to play
	ball with bro.

You see, I don't need to spell everything out. So long as I understand it, I'll be OK. Now, on to the questions.

The three short-response questions are sometimes similar to Inference questions in the multiple-choice section, in the sense that you are given a quotation from the story and then asked to infer its meaning. Here are some sample short-response questions for *The Beautiful Summer Day*, assuming that we have listened to it and will now use our notes to help us.

> O Loquacious Kahuna, this section of the test would be so easy for me if I were allowed to use all nine of my arms. Curse these simple humanoid bodies!

1. At first, Margaret does not want to play softball, but then she does. What makes her change her mind? Use details and information from the story to support your answer.

2. At the beginning of the story, Margaret is excited about college, but she is also nervous. Why is she nervous about something she wants to do? Do you think her feelings change by the end of the story? Use details and information from the story to support your answer.

3. How is the note from Margaret's mother important to the story? Use details and information from the story to support your answer.

For all of these questions, a long, one-sentence answer might suffice, but your answer will be more complete if you write 2–4 sentences. Remember, you have about five minutes to answer each question. There's no need to rush, but there's also no time to dawdle. Make sure to include key facts from the story.

To earn the maximum number of points on question 1, you would need to write 2–4 sentences describing what made Margaret change her mind. You would mention her phone conversation with Teresa, as well as how finding a music-related job changed Margaret's attitude.

For question 2, describe why Margaret is nervous about college—it's very competitive (fear of failure) and expensive. Paraphrasing things into your own words shows that you actually thought about the question. Finish up by talking about how the phone call with Teresa helped ease her nervousness, and list the reasons it did so.

Willy: You mean something like, "The phone call helped Margaret because not only did she get a job, but it was a musical gig, which meant it would improve her chances of getting into music school"?

Angela: Excellent. You used information from the passage and also explained how the information affected Margaret. You could even tack on the fact that having a good friend move to town helped improve Margaret's mood.

After the three short-responses, you'll see a "Planning Page" for the extended-responses. After you read the extended-response question, spend about five minutes planning out your response. For example, the question might look like this:

4.   Do you think Margaret is lucky or do you believe there is more to her good fortune? Use information from the story to support your answer.

You might think that on the extended-response questions, there's only one correct answer. This would be true for multiple-choice questions, but here, what matters is how well you can express yourself. Most important, if you can support your answers with examples from the story, then they'll be correct.

This is also true for the short-response questions, but you really need to understand it for the extended-response question.

Strategy

On open-ended questions, there is no set right or wrong answer. If you can support your answer with examples from the story, then it's correct.

Daniel: So if, for question 4, I wrote that Margaret's just lucky, and I pointed to the phone call coming from out of the blue—that would be accurate?

Angela: Yes, but I could also write a response saying that the phone call would never have occurred if Margaret hadn't played with Teresa at camp, so that it wasn't completely luck. Either way, we'll back up our claims with information in the passage, which is what your answer will be judged on.

After planning your response for about five minutes, write out your answer neatly (graders won't grade what they cannot read) in ten minutes. Be sure to leave a few minutes at the end to check for spelling and grammar errors. Also, check to see that you didn't omit any words the first time by mistake.

Reading and Open-Ended Questions

Angela: Day 2 of the test starts off with a long reading passage, such as a 900-word nonfiction passage, followed by two short-response questions. Then, there's a second reading passage on a subject related to the first passage, followed by one short-response question. For instance, if the first passage talks about centipedes, then the second passage would discuss the differences between centipedes and millipedes.

The three short-response questions in this section test to see how well you can understand a passage and then write about it in your own words. Remember that here, you can refer to the passage as needed, like an open-book test, but that the answers need to be in short-response form.

Ridley: It seems to me that how well we do on this section depends on whether we use the different techniques from the earlier sessions. I mean, if I'm used to referring to the passage for the multiple-choice questions, then referring to answer the open-ended questions should be second nature. And if I get comfortable with the idea of writing out answers in my own words (supported, of course, by facts from the text), then this section is just more of the same.

Angela: Yes, Ridley, the same techniques you applied on day 1 will help you perform well on day 2.

Recalling the New York State Learning Standards listed at the beginning of this chapter, the Reading and Open-Ended Questions part of the ELA exam tests how well you can analyze information and come up with a conclusion. This means that the extended-response essay in this section will ask you to do two main things: Use information from BOTH reading passages, and make some conclusions and support them with details.

> ### Information
>
> The section of the test that asks you to read two related passages and write open-ended answers is meant to see how well you are able to analyze information and come up with a conclusion. Therefore, the extended-response question in this section will ask you to do two main things:
>
> 1. Use information from both reading passages; and
>
> 2. Draw some conclusions and support them with details.

For This Listening Activity . . .	Spend This Amount of Time
Reading the first passage	5 minutes
Answering 2 short responses	5 minutes each
Reading the second passage and answering 1 short response	10 minutes
Planning and writing extended response	15 minutes
Checking work	5 minutes

The extended-response question might ask, "Explain whether you would prefer to have centipedes or millipedes living in your backyard." It doesn't matter whether you choose centipedes or millipedes, it only matters that you write convincingly about why you prefer one insect over the other.

Since you can flip around through the different pages, use the text whenever necessary, which for the most part means for every question. Why trust your memory for a key fact when the source is readily available? During the essay planning stage, when you're gathering facts to support your main idea, you should flip between the two passages and the planning page repeatedly.

Whew! This has a been a long study group! Since Willy is going to talk about the composition, why don't we call it a day and start his discussion next time?

O Most Viscous One, since I already had a date to the Spring Ball, I stopped taking notes. I was going with the captain of the women's volleyball team, and I even set Willy up on a blind date with Griselda Model 45C, the female android we brought with us from Kronhorst.

Everyone: Agreed.

Angela: Now, let's move on to more important business. Who has a date to the Spring Ball?

Ridley: Oh yes, that reminds me. Daniel, I think I need some extra help on the Inference questions: will you help me?

Daniel: Uh, yeah, um, you know, yeah, sure . . . um, yeah.

Overview: ELA Strategies

Strategy 1: On the multiple-choice section: work through the problems in whatever order YOU are most comfortable with. If you do answer the questions out of sequence, make sure you remember to fill in the proper ovals.

Strategy 2: The multiple-choice section is like an open-book test. There's no need to memorize any information in a given passage, since you can refer easily to the text to answer questions. Instead, read the passage to identify the main point and get a good idea of what—and where—the facts are.

Strategy 3: If you don't know what a word means, figure it out by looking at how it fits into the rest of the sentence and phrase (called context).

Strategy 4: Don't try to answer questions about supporting ideas based on what you think you remember or what looks right. Go back and look at the passage for the precise answer. It's not worth the risk of losing points.

Strategy 5: For the listening section, a passage will be read twice. You won't have time to write down every point or detail, so you'll have to approach this task strategically. The first time through, listen for the main idea. The second time through, listen for examples that support the main idea.

Strategy 6: Sometimes a listening passage will be accompanied by some unusual words and definitions that you'll need to know for the session. It's important that you look these words over early on so you'll understand them before the passage is read.

Strategy 7: On open-ended questions, there's no set right or wrong answer. If you can support your answer with examples from the story, then it's correct.

Sample Questions: English Language Arts

W. E. B. Du Bois

In 1895, twenty-seven-year-old W. E. B. Du Bois received his doctorate of philosophy from Harvard University, and thereby became the first African American to gain a graduate degree from America's oldest university. The Ph.D. was merely one achievement of Du Bois's distinguished academic career, but Du Bois is not known merely for being a good teacher and scholar. Along with Booker T. Washington, Du Bois was one of the most influential African American figures of the early 20th century, working throughout his life to help put an end to racism and prejudice in the United States.

William Edward Burghardt Du Bois was born in 1868 in the small rural Massachusetts town of Great Barrington. Du Bois quickly showed himself to be an eager, apt student, earning high marks in all of his classes. Du Bois longed to go to Harvard, but his application was not accepted. Still resolved to go to college, Du Bois worked for a year after graduating high school to earn money, and four townsfolk—including the school principal—pitched in enough money to send Du Bois to Fisk University, a prominent African American university in Tennessee. After graduating with honors from Fisk, Du Bois applied to Harvard again and was accepted. Although Harvard did not recognize his degree from Fisk, it did provide him with a grant.

After receiving his doctorate from Harvard, Du Bois eventually settled into a job as a professor at Atlanta University. While working there from 1897 to 1910, Du Bois produced his most influential piece of literature, The Souls of Black Folk. *Published in 1903, the novel frankly discusses the challenges involved with eliminating "the color line" in the United States, and critics and scholars alike instantly praised the book for its insight and candor. Du Bois went on to write more than 20 books in his life, both fiction and nonfiction.*

Du Bois did more than write books, however. Two years after The Souls of Black Folk *came out, he founded the Niagara Movement, an early equal rights movement. While the Niagara Movement floundered after a few years, Du Bois joined together with other equal-rights supporters to create the National Association for the Advancement of Colored People, or NAACP, in 1910. The NAACP remains an important social rights organization to this day.*

While at the NAACP, Du Bois became the editor of the organization's magazine The Crisis. *This magazine reached only a thousand readers in its first year of existence, but its impassioned writing and unique position—it was one of the only magazines to focus on African American issues—quickly caused its readership level to soar. Within a decade of its founding,* The Crisis *was read by over 100,000 readers, and through this magazine the NAACP was able to effectively pass on its ideals and beliefs.*

Du Bois was one of the foremost African American figures of the early 20th century, but he was by no means the only one. Booker T. Washington, founder of the Tuskegee Institute, was also a prominent character in the equality movement. While both men were deeply committed to improving the lives of African Americans in the United States, they had widely different beliefs. Du Bois believed that African Americans should speak out against prejudice whenever it occurred, and that the fight for equality would be led by college-educated African Americans. Washington, on the other hand, believed that economic independence was the key factor in the push towards equality, and that until economic disadvantages plaguing African Americans were eliminated, racial demands should not be pressed. This disagreement in philosophies caused both Du Bois and Washington to oppose each other's efforts often. Du Bois wrote several essays criticizing Washington and his beliefs, and Washington responded with attacks against Du Bois as well.

In 1934 Du Bois left as editor of The Crisis *and went back to teaching at Atlanta University. While he returned to the NAACP briefly in the 1940s, Du Bois left the United States in 1961 and went to Ghana, where the president of that country had asked him to compile a massive history of Africa. Du Bois died two years later, and was buried with honors in Ghana. The day after his death, Martin Luther King Jr. gave his famous "I have a dream" speech, a speech that helped push forward the civil rights movement that Du Bois worked all his life to bring about.*

1. Which is a FACT from the passage?

   A. Du Bois was a courageous fighter for human rights.
   B. Du Bois' first published book was *The Souls of Black Folk*.
   C. The creation of the Niagara Movement was crucial to the success of the NAACP.
   D. Du Bois graduated from Fisk University with honors.

2. The author of this passage suggests that the writings and accomplishments of W. E. B. Du Bois will probably be—

   A. awarded national honors.
   B. not very useful to future scholars of African-American history.
   C. meaningful to future generations.
   D. disregarded by modern human rights organizations.

3. The author of the passage provides evidence to suggest that *The Crisis* became a successful magazine because—

   A. at the time, it was one of the only magazines to discuss topics relevant to African Americans.
   B. the NAACP was new, and people were interested in its creation.
   C. Du Bois already had a large following who read all his works.
   D. it was read by over a 100,000 people a decade after its founding.

4. What is the main idea of this passage?

   A. Du Bois was a well-known scholar while at Harvard.
   B. Du Bois and his work on *The Crisis* helped make the NAACP an important organization.
   C. Du Bois worked throughout his life to promote racial equality.
   D. Booker Washington and Du Bois did not often agree with each other.

5. Du Bois believed that future leaders of the African American equality movement would be—

   A. armed with useful job skills.
   B. well-educated.
   C. members of the NAACP.
   D. authors.

6. The author of the passage provides evidence to suggest that Booker Washington—

   A. worked closely with Du Bois to achieve similar goals.
   B. did not approve of the creation of the NAACP.
   C. was a distinguished scholar like Du Bois.
   D. emphasized learning job skills as a key to improving the lives of African Americans.

7. Which event in the passage happened last?

   A. *The Souls of Black Folk* is released.
   B. Du Bois was asked to work on the history of Africa.
   C. Du Bois goes back to work for the NAACP.
   D. Du Bois teaches at Atlanta University.

8. Du Bois and Booker T. Washington both worked hard for social equality, yet the two men disliked each other. If both men wanted the same thing, why did they become enemies?

The Panama Canal

In 1517 the Portuguese explorer Vasco Nuñez de Balboa crossed the narrow strip of land in Central America separating the Atlantic and Pacific Oceans and became the first European to see the Pacific. He had sailed across the Atlantic looking for a water passage to China and the Far East, but was unable to find one connecting the two oceans. Had Balboa's distant relatives attempted the same voyage four hundred years later, they would have been successful, thanks to the creation of the Panama Canal in 1914.

Extending just over 50 miles, the Panama Canal is a waterway that connects Limon Bay, in the Atlantic Ocean, to the Bay of Panama, on the Pacific side. The canal allows ships to bypass sailing around all of South America, cutting about 7,800 miles off the typical voyage. Since it is such a time-saving measure, about 13,000 ships use the Panama Canal each year, carrying huge amounts of cargo. Although the canal is still used by many ships, today's oil supertankers are too big to use the canal, and its military use has been limited due to the fact that today's large aircraft carriers are also unable to fit through it.

Like the Great Wall of China, the Panama Canal is one of the world's great feats of engineering. However, achieving such an arduous task did not come easily, and many early attempts failed badly. The first attempt to create a transoceanic canal came in 1878, when Frenchman Lucien Napoleon Bonaparte Wyse received permission from Colombia to build a canal across Panama. (At the time, Panama was a territory of Colombia.) Wyse gave his construction rights over to another Frenchman, Ferdinand De Lesseps, whose company had worked on the Suez Canal in Egypt. Lesseps's company started digging in 1882, but soon encountered a host of problems. The group did not have the proper digging tools, dishonest politicians stole vast amounts of money that were supposed to be used toward the building effort, and to make matters worse, tropical diseases, such as malaria and yellow fever, killed hundreds of workers. Seven years after they started digging, Lesseps's company went bankrupt.

During the Spanish-American War of 1898, an American warship on the West Coast had to take the long journey around South America in order to bolster the Atlantic Fleet. This delayed journey helped convince the United States Congress that the creation of a canal would be important for national defense. By 1904 the United States gained control of the building rights to the Panama Canal. The United States achieved this by backing Panama's push for independence. In return for America's support, Panama gave the United States exclusive control of a 10-mile strip of land.

Once work on the canal resumed, the most important person was not an engineer, but a physician. Doctor William Gorgas, an American colonel, spent the first two years instituting methods to help eliminate tropical disease from the area. Since diseases such as malaria are carried by mosquitoes, Gorgas made workers drain the swamps where mosquitoes bred and clear away large patches of brush and grass where the mosquitoes swarmed. He also led a program to exterminate rats, which are carriers of bubonic plague. By reducing the disease rate, work on the canal could proceed at a better pace.

Ten years after the United States began work on the project, the Panama Canal was complete. A landslide closed the canal briefly in 1915-1916, but since then the canal has functioned without interruption. Although the United States was granted exclusive control of the Panama Canal in 1904, the United States and Panama soon started negotiating over control of the canal. The two sides were at an impasse for many years, but in 1977 the *two governments agreed on a treaty that would give control of the land around the canal back to Panama in 1979. The agreement also stated that canal operations would be handed over to the Panamanian government on December 31, 1999.*

Today, work still continues on the Panama Canal, as various areas are widened to allow more ships through at one time. Today, if Balboa were to sail from Portugal in search of China, he could look over the side of his ship as it passes from the Atlantic Ocean to the Pacific Ocean and view the progress himself.

9. The word *arduous* in this passage means—

   A. gigantic.
   B. simple.
   C. impossible.
   D. difficult.

10. What is the main idea of this passage?

   A. The Panama Canal was difficult to build because of many tropical diseases.
   B. The Panama Canal took a long time to complete but has since been very useful.
   C. The independence of Panama helped the United States build the canal.
   D. Most great feats of engineering take a long time to complete.

11. In the passage, the word *impasse* means—

   A. deadlock.
   B. state of confusion.
   C. agreement.
   D. state of hostility.

12. Dr. William Gorgas can best be described as—

   A. hopeful.
   B. ingenious.
   C. calm.
   D. thrifty.

13. Which is an OPINION in this passage?

   A. The Panama Canal connects Limon Bay to the Bay of Panama.
   B. Many canal workers died because of tropical diseases.
   C. Balboa would be surprised to see how his idea of the canal was made a reality.
   D. Improvements are still being made to the Panama Canal.

14. While working on the Panama Canal, Ferdinand De Lesseps most likely—

   A. experienced great frustration.
   B. gained enormous wealth.
   C. achieved international respect.
   D. sacrificed personal relationships.

15. The passage suggests that during the 21st century the operation of the canal will be in the hands of—

   A. the United States.
   B. Colombia.
   C. France.
   D. Panama.

16. What were some of the causes for the delay of the creation of the Panama Canal?

17. How are Dr. William Gorgas's struggles similar to the struggles of W. E. B. Du Bois, from the previous reading passage?

The Fine Arts Fair

Lana carried her painting out of her house and gently placed it in the back seat of her parent's car. Today was the day of the Throckmorton Fine Arts Fair, and it was the first year Lana had entered a painting into the competition. Most of the people who went to the show were merely curious, but there were several people who bought one or two paintings every year. Even more importantly, a group of art professors from Florida State University awarded one painter and one sculptor each the title of "Top New Artist of the Year." While the honor itself was worth the entry fee of five dollars, the winners of the award would also receive one free art class over the summer at the University of Paris.

Her heart was racing as Lana glanced down at the program sheet to see the schedule of events.

23rd Annual Throckmorton Fine Arts Fair
Sponsored by the Throckmorton Arts Department

March 22, 2000

Location: Busy Bee Garden Complex, 505 Busy Bee Boulevard

Time: Fair opens at 9:00 A.M. to the public. Contestants displaying their art should arrive 30 minutes before the gates open. The fair will close at 4:00 P.M.

Artwork: Sculptures will be on display at the east lawn of the complex. Paintings will be displayed in both the Merriweather Room and the Phlox Room.

Food: Refreshments will be served at the concession stand near the east lawn. At noon, lunch will be provided by Artz House of Barbecue. Lunch is free for all artists with pieces on display, and $3.00 for everyone else. Visitors are asked not to take any food or drink inside the complex.

Directions: Starting at Throckmorton High School, take the Mulberry Highway west until the Bluebonnet Trail exit. Turn left onto Bluebonnet Trail, and then turn right at Busy Bee Boulevard, which is the third stop light after leaving the highway. (The streets that you will pass after you exit the highway are Granger and Musth, in that order.)

18. What is the main purpose of the program sheet?

    A. It gives the time the fair opens.
    B. It provides directions to the site of the fair.
    C. It gives details about where the artwork is displayed and other necessary information.
    D. It provides a detailed discussion of what foods will be served.

19. The passage gives you reason to believe that the Throckmorton Fine Arts Fair—

    A. has been going on since 1968.
    B. is very close to the high school.
    C. is one of the largest art fairs in the area.
    D. has always been held at the Busy Bee Garden Complex.

20. According to the program sheet, where will Lana's painting be placed?

    A. the east lawn of the complex
    B. the Merriweather Room
    C. the Merriweather or the Phlox Room
    D. the Phlox Room

21. If Lana arrives at the fair at 9:30, then she will be—

    A. thirty minutes late.
    B. one hour late.
    C. two hours early for lunch.
    D. right on time.

22. Which of these best describes Lana?

    A. nervous but excited
    B. agitated and frightful
    C. anxious and pessimistic
    D. enthusiastic and arrogant

23. Which of these is a FACT given in the passage?

    A. Lunch will cost Lana $3.00.
    B. Granger and Musth street intersect each other.
    C. Sculptures may be seen in the Phlox Room.
    D. To get from the garden complex to the high school, at some point you could drive on Bluebonnet Trail and then take Mulberry Highway east.

24. A friend of yours is interested in going to the Throckmorton Arts Fair and wishes to participate in as many activities and events as possible. Write out a brief description of what a person could do while at the Fair.

English Language Arts: Composition

Session Leader: Willy H_2SO_4

O Your Pookiness, our fourth meeting was going to be held in Willy's garage, but it seems Willy's parents have asked him to never set foot in the garage again. We held the meeting in Willy's old treehouse instead, which was quite cozy.
—X!Frumious

NAME: William Bruce Walker, better known as Willy H_2SO_4

BORN: February 17, 1989
Chautauqua, New York

NOTES: A chemistry buff, Willy once made soap from materials he collected on a Boy Scout nature trip into the Catskills. He then wrote the essay, "How Cleaning Your Hands at the top of a mountain is a Character-Building Experience," which earned him the Best Essay of the Year from his grade school. A garage accident also earned Willy his nickname, although sulfuric acid was not actually used. He owns one pet, a coati mundi name Heisenberg.

Daniel: This treehouse is amazingly decorated. I love the stuffed moose you have in the corner.

Willy: It wasn't easy to get him up the tree, but it was well worth it. I want to bring up a small piano next, but my parents aren't thrilled about the idea.

Let's get down to business, shall we?

The Essay

The last part of the English Language Arts test requires you to write an essay. You'll have roughly 45 minutes to complete the essay, since this section is the second half of a 90 minute session.

Daniel: What's the deal with the grading on the ELA section? The Math test has definite point totals, but I haven't heard anything like that about the ELA test.

Willy: There are no number totals for ELA. In essence, there's only one score that matters on this part of the exam, and it's a scaled score from 1 to 4. This number is intended to show how well you are progressing on the standards upon which the Regents Exam is based, something you'll need to pass in order to graduate high school. The NYSED breakdown is as follows:

Score Levels on NYS 8ᵗʰ Grade ELA Composition

Level 4	*You have exceeded performance standards and should get high marks on the Regents Examination.*
Level 3	*You have met performance standards and with continued effort, should pass the Regents Exam.*
Level 2	*You will need extra help in order to pass the Regents Exam.*
Level 1	*You have serious academic deficiencies.*

A variety of factors is used to determine your score. The multiple-choice questions are graded by a computer but teachers grade your written responses and essay.

Ridley: That process seems a little arbitrary.

Willy: It might seem that way, but it isn't really. The readers are experienced at reading these essays and assigning grades, so you don't need to worry about your essay suffering if a reader slams his foot in his car door that morning.

All of the listening and reading questions will receive a grade of 0–6, while the essay will receive a grade of 0–3. There's also a Mechanics grade of 0–3, which judges your punctuation and grammar on the essay and both extended responses.

Ridley: Huh?

Willy: Look at the scoring chart on the following page, but keep in mind that the numbers themselves are not quite as important as they are on the math test.

ELA Section	Total Possible Points
Session 1	
Part 1 *(25 multiple-choice questions)*	*0–25*
Part 2 *(listening passage)*	*0–6*
Session 2	
Part 1 *(reading/writing section)*	*0–6*
Part 2 *(essay)*	*0–3*
Mechanics *(essay and 2 extended responses)*	*0–3*

You can't add these scoring points up, so don't even try it. The entire ELA test is graded holistically, so while you could crunch numbers this way, the people who grade the exam aren't; they will base your score of 1–4 on whether your exam has "exceeded, met, or failed to meet the standards set for this test."

Angela: My brain hurts.

Willy: I didn't say the system was easy. Just remember there's only one real score we're interested, and that's the 1–4 score for the entire ELA Test. However, since the essay is scored from 0–3 and your mechanics level is scored from 0–3, I'll talk about the essay scoring on a 0 to 6 scale. Granted, this isn't exactly accurate, but for our purposes here, since the mechanics score will be mostly based on your essay, we'll approach it that way. Test purists will have to forgive me.

6 is the highest score, while a score of 0 means that the essay was incomprehensible, or way off topic, such as when you have written a letter to the Mayor of New York demanding that the Seven Dwarves be allowed to have special parking permits when you were asked to write about the pros or cons of traffic rules.

Readers use a holistic scoring method to determine your score, based on the following categories.

ELA Objective	What it Means
1. **Meaning**	How well does the paper present and maintain a clear theme or idea?
2. **Organization**	Is there a coherent structure to the development of the essay, such as a beginning, middle, and end? Are transitions used properly? Is there a conclusion?
3. **Development**	What is the quality of the details used to support the main idea? Are the details credible, thorough, and elaborate?
4. **Language Use**	Does the essay have proper punctuation, spelling, capitalization, and variation in sentence structure?

Now, you might think, "the essay is worth 6 points, and there are four objectives. That means I get a 1.5 points for each objective, right?"

X!Frumious: Sounds good to me.

Willy: Sounds good, but it's wrong. While all four objectives are important, the information you provide to support your main idea (Objective 3) is the most important factor in your essay score.

Of course, if you don't have the other objectives down pat, the amount of supporting information you provide is irrelevant. In other words, if you haven't kept on the topic you're supposed to write about (Objective 1), you're heading for a score of 0. And if don't organize your thoughts into an introduction, main body, and conclusion (Objective 2), but just write whatever comes to mind—that should earn you a score of between 0 and 1. Same thing if you don't use English in a comprehensible manner (Objective 4).

> **Strategy**
>
> While you should do your best to meet all four writing objectives, the most important factor in your essay score will be how well you use information to support your main idea (Objective 3).

Angela: I understand the first two points you made, but how do you define "English in a comprehensible manner"? I'm fortunate to be a foreigner who speaks English well, but I know that I am an exception, rather than the rule.

Willy: That's true, Angela, but the key is to write English well enough to be understood. If you write the sentence "People should not to be out after curfew hours," it won't matter that you have improper verb phrasing in the predicate because the sentence is still comprehensible. The key is to justify why "people should not to be out after curfew." There would, however, be a problem if the above statement looked like "people out after curfew." In this sentence fragment, there's no point being made, and this essay would suffer.

Improper grammar may prevent you from getting a 6 on the essay, but it won't stop you from getting an adequate score.

While poor grammar won't kill your essay, poor supporting details will. To illustrate the various levels of detail that an essay could have, look at the chart below.

How Your Essay is Evaluated

Level of Detail	Description
Extended response (weakest)	You have linked your main idea to one piece of information, which begins to clarify your meaning.
Somewhat elaborated	You have provided additional information that further clarifies your meaning.
Moderately elaborated	You have clarified your main idea in even greater detail, through the use of additional illustrations, anecdotes, and examples.
Fully elaborated (strongest)	You have provided thorough, clear, and convincing support for your main idea. You provide a logical progression of reasons, use effective transitions, and offer substantial and specific support.

Do your best to write a fully elaborated essay—that means you should not only provide supporting details, but you should explain how those details connect. Keep your ideas simple and sensible, as complicated ideas are harder to explain and support.

As you write, don't assume anything on the part of the reader. Explain *why* the supporting information is significant. You want to build an argument from beginning to end, after all. Lastly, don't provide information that you know little about. Your writing will be far more skillful and persuasive if you stick to issues that you're comfortable with.

The Writing Prompt

Willy: Now that you have some idea about the grading and structure behind the essay, let's talk about the essay itself. On the test, you'll see a prompt—a statement of some sort followed by the question, "What is your position regarding this issue?" Here's a sample prompt for us to work on.

> **Strategy**
>
> *As long as your English is understandable, imperfect grammar won't cripple your essay. Poor supporting details, however, will.*

> Recently the local school board was given control of large plot of land directly behind the school's baseball field. Some members of the Student Council are recommending to the school board that the land should be made into a park.

> What is your position concerning this issue? Write a letter to the president of your school board stating your point of view and supporting it with convincing reasons. Be sure to explain your reasons in detail.

Now, your first con-sideration is, do you support the park plan or not? It doesn't matter what side of the argument you take. All that matters is how *well* you support your argument.

Ridley: So "I like the park idea" is not the correct answer?

Willy: Right, and "I do not like the park idea" isn't correct, either. What you are aiming for is a well-supported argument vs. a poorly-supported argument. Once you have decided on what position you'll take, start planning your essay.

Notice I didn't say, "start writing your essay." The key to any good essay is thorough planning, so don't just start writing frantically. Remember, your goal isn't to set a new record by finishing the essay in five minutes.

As you plan your essay, I suggest numbering each reason you come up with, and then developing each one into fuller detail and explanation. Let's say my main statement is, "I like fresh fruit better than rotten fruit." I should now come up with several connected reasons that explain why I like fresh fruit.

Ridley: You want to come up with *at least* four reasons in order to complete the four different stages of elaboration you mentioned earlier, right?

Willy: Exactly. If I said only, "I like fresh fruit because it tastes good," then I'd get only an extended response, and I'm shooting for fully elaborated. Therefore, in my planning stage I would write on a scratch sheet of paper:

Use Your Time Wisely

Planning essay About 10 minutes

Writing About 30 minutes

Revising and proofreading About 5 minutes

Main idea: I like fresh fruit better than rotten fruit.

1. Fresh fruit tastes better than rotten fruit, so I'll probably enjoy fresh fruit more.

2. Since I enjoy eating fresh fruit, I eat a lot of it, and since it's nutritious, I improve my health by doing so.

3. Rotten fruit could have diseases or bacteria that would make me sick, while with fresh fruit that probably would not happen.

4. Fresh fruit is easier to find, since most stores don't sell rotten fruit (though I could buy fresh fruit and then let it rot, but it would take a while.)

5. Some types of rotting fruit eventually become foods of their own, such as grapes changing into raisins, but if I wanted to eat raisins I'd buy a box of raisins, and if I wanted to eat grapes, I'd buy fresh grapes.

I'm just in the planning stage, so some reasons will be better than others. I was just brainstorming ideas. Looking over them, reason 1 is good, and because reason 2 links into it, they're two good additional pieces of infor-mation. Reason 3 is pretty good, but it would be better to explain that idea some more. Reasons 4 and 5 are helpful because they show I'm trying to look at both sides of the argument. In

---

Information

Don't plan your essay on the two lined pages provided in the test booklet, since that space is needed for the essay and nothing else. Use the separate sheet provided to jot down notes instead.

---

reason 5, I take the pro-rotten fruit side and claim that some rotting foods become foods of their own, but then I quickly refute that and reinforce my original idea.

The more reasons you can come with, the better, so long as they help prove your point. But it's just as important to link your reasons together—such as reasons 1 and 2 above. How do they all flow? You need to make sense of your ideas so the reader can get a clear idea of what you are saying. The planning stage is where you make or break your essay, so take the time to come up with as many compelling reasons as you can. If you come up with 15 reasons, decide which are the best ones, and then figure out how they all fit together. Also, figure out who your audience is, so you can choose the appropriate words and tone. What you would write to your school principal would probably be different from what you would write to your classmates. Then, compose your essay.

> **Strategy**
>
> *Always try to present an under-standing of both sides of the argument. If you can describe the other side's position and reasons why you disagree with it, you'll strengthen your argument and boost your essay.*

To guide you through a mock essay, let's look again at the writing prompt about the proposed park.

> Recently the local school board was given control of large plot of land directly behind the school's baseball field. Some members of the Student Council are recommending to the school board that the land should be made into a park.
>
> What is your position concerning this issue? Write a letter to the president of your school board stating your point of view and supporting it with convincing reasons. Be sure to explain your reasons in detail.

My first question will be, "Do I want to support the park idea or not?" In this case, I'm not going to support the Student Council position. Instead, I'll offer my own proposal for how to use the land. I believe an organic vegetable garden would be a better idea.

Now that I've decided what position I'll choose, it's time to brainstorm reasons. Here are some of my notes.

<u>Ideas for Organic Vegetable Farm Essay</u>

1. Offers a variety of unique learning opportunities in both farming and science.

2. Gives students a good reason to be outside on a beautiful day.

3. Sale of vegetables could be used to fund field trips and other activities.

4. Hands-on experience in farming could give students a helpful advantage in summer internships.

5. Vegetable sale can be run as a business, giving people work experience.

6. Students on detention can pick weeds.

7. No other school has an organic vegetable farm, making us stand out.

8. New school mascot: Binky, the additive-free rutabaga.

The next step is to decide on the best sequence to put these ideas in. I know that it's important to provide fully elaborated reasons in my essay, so I know I shouldn't just write out these eight ideas in the order I thought of them. Looking them over, I think I can group some of the related points. For instance, I think Ideas 1, 4, and 5 are closely connected, since they all related to using the farm for learning purposes. I could write a paragraph in my essay that looks something like this:

Dear School Board President,

Instead of using the vacant space next to the school for a park, I would like to suggest an alternate use. There are currently numerous parks throughout the city, and while everyone enjoys green spaces, I believe we could do better here at Eastbury High. That's right: I'm thinking what you're thinking—let's start an organic vegetable farm.

Having an organic vegetable farm would provide a wealth of learning opportunities for our students. Students in botany could get hands-on experience dealing with plants and how they grow, something that I believe most other high school students don't get in their schools. Science students could also use the garden to learn more about genetics, as they could combine plants with different traits to see what occurs. Students could also eat the vegetables grown in the garden, or even sell them in order to raise money for school activities, like field trips and school dances. If you put students in charge of selling the produce, then they would gain

> valuable business experience, learning all about the sale and pricing of fruits and vegetables.

I could go on with this paragraph, but I think you get the point. On the real essay I would definitely continue on, because the more related points I can string together, the closer my chances are that I reach full elaboration.

Daniel: But what about the other ideas? I don't see how you're going to attach the mascot idea to anything.

Willy: Then I won't use it. I don't have to use all the ideas I first thought of, and if I come up with anything while I'm writing, I can always include that.

One other paragraph I should include in my essay is one in which I look at the possible objections to having an organic garden, and then reject them one by one. This shows I understand both sides of the argument.

> I know that there are many close-minded people out there who have always been against the marriage of schools and organic farms. They might claim that learning about farming is pointless since most high school students will never farm in their lives, and even those who do become real farmers will do so on massive farms that use computerized harvesters and automated sprinklers. Anyone who claims that learning about farming is pointless is missing the entire point of education, which is to learn things and become a better person. Maybe none of us will become farmers. So what? That shouldn't stop us from having gardens of our own when we are older and growing our own vegetables, which are almost always superior to grocery store produce in size and quality.

> What better way to instill a spirit of pride in a school than to do something new and unusual? School morale is important—having an organic garden would set us apart from other schools, and school spirit would become very visible. Having a mascot like "Binky the Additive-free Rutabaga" is not very threatening, but at least it's accurate. I happen to know for a fact that our current mascot, the tiger, has never roamed the lands around Eastbury High.

Finally, before you start writing out your essay, there is one last thing you need to bear in mind: penmanship. Make sure your handwriting is neat. Make it easy for the graders to read your handwriting, or your essay score will suffer.

Any final questions about the essay? Good.

Overview: ELA Essay

Step 1: Think

- First, plan your essay. Brainstorm ideas, writing down whatever comes to your mind in support of your point. Use numbers to list your points, elaborating on every idea.

- Select your best ideas and decide how to clearly connect them together. Your goal is to persuade your audience of your point of view. Your essay must flow, so use transition words and ideas to link your ideas.

- Use language and tone that are appropriate for your audience.

- Take a strong stand **for** or **against** the idea expressed in the prompt.

Step 2: Write

- Your essay should be 3–4 paragraphs in length. It should contain an introduction, a body, and a conclusion.

- Introduction: States your argument and briefly describes the reasons you will provide in support of that argument.

- Body paragraph(s): Explains the reasons behind your argument. Support your reasons with facts and examples. If you decide on one long body paragraph, make sure that it's clear to the reader where one reason ends and the next begins.

- Conclusion: Briefly restates your argument and the reasons behind it, using somewhat different language.

Step 3: Repair

- Your first draft is not your final draft. Once you've finished writing your essay, revise and proofread it.

- Neatness counts!—make certain that your handwriting is legible.

Science and Technology Assessment

Session Leader: Willy H_2SO_4

O Most Calibrated One, our fifth meeting was back at Willy's treehouse. At first, I was going to skip this meeting, since what more do I need to know about science & technology? I mean, I have a spaceship capable of interstellar travel, and I know everything there is to know about Squarcinos—the gregarious, fun-loving subatomic particles that make up all matter in the universe. Well, then I found out that Squarcinos were not going to be on these exams, as earthlings are still enamored of such outdated concepts as "mass," "time," "gravity," and even "sound." How quaint! Here are my notes.
—X!Frumious

NAME: William Bruce Walker

ADDITIONAL NOTES: A born inventor, Willy almost won a grade school science fair with a scale-model replica of Mount Vesuvius and the town of Pompeii. Unfortunately, Willy tried to use real lava—or at least to get the lava/ketchup running out of Mount Vesuvius as hot as possible for realism's sake—which did not quite work as planned. However, the black smoke and the smell of burning ketchup did make an impressive spectacle, and he was awarded second place (first place went to a girl whose display did not trigger the fire sprinklers).

Science Test

Willy: Ah, the world of science. A world of cool logic, precise calculations, and fascinating discoveries. What could be better than that?

Angela: How about a world of *free money*?

Ridley: Or a world of *world peace*?

X!Frumious: Or a world of *fruit-chewy morsels*?

Daniel: Better yet, a world where *everyone thinks Daniel is totally the best*?

Willy: Those are all fine options, and when there's a section of the test that deals with fruit-chewy morsels, I'll be happy to learn all about it. Until then . . .

How the Science Test Adds Up

Willy: The Grade 8 Science exam has a rather involved format. Since familiarity helps your confidence, make sure you feel comfortable with all the various twists and turns. The breakdown is as follows:

Overview: NYS 8th Grade Science test

Session 1 (Written Portion)	**Part A**	Answer 17 multiple-choice questions
	Part B	Answer 17 questions of mixed format
	Part C	Answer 11 open-response questions
Session 2 (Laboratory Portion)		Spend 15 minutes at each of three lab stations, performing various scientific tasks
Time		2 hours for Session 1 1 hour for Session 2

Session 1, the written portion of the test, lasts two hours and consists of three parts. For part A, you'll have to answer some multiple-choice questions. For part B, you'll answer some multiple-choice and some short-response question. The short-response questions are like fill-in-the blank questions; for example, with a graph question, you would have to write out an answer choice rather than select from existing choices.

Part C will have the hardest questions. They'll be multi-part questions that will often require you to perform several tasks. Some questions will be fairly straightforward, while others will require extensive reading.

Session 2, the laboratory portion of the test, accounts for 15 percent of your score. It consists of three different lab stations where you'll have to accomplish various tasks.

As on the other subject tests, the open-ended science questions will take a lot of time, even though they'll account for just over half of your overall grade. So it's a good strategy to do all the easier multiple-choice questions before you attack the open-ended ones.

Willy: The Science test is designed to test students in five major skills areas of the New York Science Core Curriculum. According to the New York State Education Department, these five standards are:

Standards		Percentage on the Test
1.	Mathematical Analysis, Scientific Inquiry, and Technological Design	20–25%
2.	Information Systems	0–5%
3.	The Living Environment; The Physical Setting	65–75%
4.	Interconnectedness: Common Themes	0–5%
5.	Interdisciplinary Problem Solving	0–10%

Willy: Looking at the chart above, does anything stand out?

Ridley: It looks like standard 3 is the one to focus your studies on.

Willy: You have that right, Ridley. Although there are five content strands, strand 1 (which I'll shorten and call *Inquiry* from now on) and strand 3 (which includes biology, physical science, and earth & space science) make up a huge portion of the test. Since at least two-thirds of the test will be on the categories I just mentioned, make sure you know those areas before Test Day.

Strategy

Focus on brushing up your science skills in biology, physical science, and earth & space science, and worry less about information systems.

Willy: A quick discussion of POE is useful before jumping into the particulars of each standards. On the Science test, using your head can take you a long way, so make sure you don't get flustered and think that you need some high-falutin science knowledge in order to do well.

Consider a question asking about shadows. Do you need schooling in optics to know that the longest shadows occur when the sun is lowest, and that shadows are shortest when the sun is high?

Ridley: No, I know that fact from experience: Football practice sometimes runs late, and as the sun sets my cheerleading shadow is about 30 feet long.

Willy: Therefore, Ridley, you don't need to know everything about optics to answer this question.

1. A person is standing in an open field during the summer. Sunrise is at 6:43 A.M. that day, while sunset is at 8:52 P.M. At what time will this person's shadow be the longest?

   A. 7:42 A.M.
   B. 9:02 P.M.
   C. 1:04 A.M.
   D. 1:04 P.M.

Ridley: B and C are wrong because the sun won't be out. With D, the sun should be almost overhead, so it won't cast much of a shadow. That leaves A.

Willy: Good job. Remember, the Science test will contain more questions involving common sense than will the other subject tests.

Throughout this section, I'll try to mention other times when common sense and POE can help you answer a question. For now, let's talk about standards and question types.

Information

While there are precise scientific explanations for most of the questions, simply understanding the basic scientific principles and applying common sense will often work just as well.

Overall Science Topics

Inquiry

Multiple-choice Inquiry questions primarily ask you to determine the best way to set up an experiment. Open-response Inquiry questions, on the other hand, ask you to set up the experiment.

2. Jonas wants to find out if the rainfall in his town is becoming acid rain. The best way for him to collect this information would be to

    A. gather one sample on one rainy day.
    B. gather one sample on several rainy days.
    C. gather several samples on one rainy day.
    D. gather several samples on several rainy days.

3. Jennifer made several small parachutes by cutting out different-sized triangles of cloth, and then tying string to each of the three corners. The corners were then tied to one or more pens. Next she held each parachute 3 meters above the ground, dropped it, and measured the time it took to fall to the ground.

    a. Identify one factor that would affect the time of a parachute's fall.
    b. Predict the relationship between the factor you identified and the time of fall.
    c. Describe an experiment you could try that would test your prediction.

Willy: To answer these questions completely, you'll need to have a good idea of the best way to run an experiment. Here are some pointers in that area:

1. *In any experiment, you want to be able to isolate one factor by keeping all other factors constant.* (The Latin term for this *ceteris paribum*, meaning "all other things equal.") That way, you can be certain that any changes that occur are because of the one factor you have isolated.

Angela: So if I want to test how the size of the parachute affects its rate of fall, I would make sure to keep the weight (the number of pens) equal.

Willy: Yes, and if possible, you would want the cloth to be the same material, the wind to be the same speed, the temperature to be equal for each time—ideally, all factors other than parachute size should be constant each time.

> 2. *The more relevant data you can collect* (over a longer period of time), *the better.*

Daniel: On question 2, then, the best answer is D, since Jonas would have the largest number of samples.

Willy: Right. The more information you have, the better you can prove an experiment. If Jonas had only one rain sample, who's to say that there couldn't be something strange about that sample? Or if he had several samples from only one day, perhaps something occurred that one day to throw his readings off. But if he had numerous samples over a period of time, and they all showed the same thing, then Jonas could make a more accurate prediction.

> 3. *For some experiments, using a control group allows you to judge the effects of an introduced variable.*

A control group is a way of ensuring Point 1, *ceteris paribum*. Let's say we wanted to prove that ketchup helps tomato plants grow. To set up a proper experiment, we would start out with two identical tomato plants in identical surroundings (soil, light, and so forth). Then, we would add ketchup to one of the plants, and judge its rate of growth against the plant that does not get ketchup. The plant that doesn't get ketchup is the control group.

Ridley: I get it. If you didn't have a control plant, there would be no way to know exactly what effect ketchup has on the tomato plant. Sure, it could grow 10 inches, but we wouldn't know exactly what caused it to grow. But with a control plant that grew 8 inches, and a ketchup-fed plant that grew 10 inches, you could conclude that ketchup caused the plant to grow an extra two inches.

Willy: Right. Be sure you know how to set up an experiment, because the odds are excellent that there will be one open-response question asking you to do just that.

Also, some science questions will ask you to look read data in a chart or graph. If this sounds familiar to you, it should, since these questions are exactly like the chart questions on the Math test.

Information

Answering a chart or graph question on the Science test is the same as answering a chart or graph question on the Math test.

Willy: This just illustrates how learning a technique on one test can often help you on another one.

Physical Sciences

Willy: Physical Science questions deal with the world around us. There are questions about electricity, heat, gravity, sunlight, evaporation, and how light waves travel. Having a basic understanding of all those items will help you do well on these problems, so don't worry about the exact scientific knowledge if you don't know it.

4. Lime juice has a pH lower than 7, is corrosive, and tastes sour. Lime juice is classified as

   A. an element.
   B. an acid.
   C. a base.
   D. More information is needed to classify lime juice.

You don't need to understand what "pH lower than 7" means in order to get this question right. Granted, if you do, the question becomes fairly simple, but if you don't, we can still find the answer. Any ideas?

Daniel: I eliminated A, since I know what an element is, as well as D, since that's the kind of answer a student who doesn't understand the question would pick. That leaves B and C.

Angela: I picked B because the question says lime juice is "corrosive," and I know that acids eat away, or corrode, things.

Ridley: I picked B because I read the label of some limeade drink, and it said one of the main ingredients was "citric acid."

Willy: B is right, for all those reasons. Those were some good guesses. Here's another question.

5. A laser beam shines on a mirror at the angle shown above. Which diagram shows what will happen to the beam after it strikes the mirror?

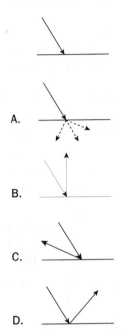

A.

B.

C.

D.

Ooh, lasers! What happens when light strikes a mirror—does it go through it?

Daniel: Uh, no.

Willy: Then A is wrong. So now, let's just decide which answer choice looks like the best answer. Think about how, when you throw a ball at a wall, it bounces off at the opposite angle. That principle would probably hold up on this question as well.

Daniel: Then the answer is D.

Biology, Also Called Life Sciences in Certain Circles

Willy: Biology questions test how well you know the traits and habits of animals and plants. Do you understand a basic food chain, with the little guys getting eaten by the big guys? If so, you'll do well in this section, or in corporate finance. Some common biology themes are photosynthesis, parts of a cell, and heredity.

6. In human beings, brown eyes are dominant over green eyes. If a pure brown-eyed man has a child with a pure green-eyed women, what color will their child's eyes be?

A. definitely blue
B. definitely brown
C. probably brown but perhaps blue
D. probably blue but perhaps brown

Willy: If you were to take a guess on this question, you might like C, since it hedges your bet. Sure, it's probably brown, but why not leave yourself an "out"? But in genetics, that doesn't happen. Here are some key genetic points:

1. Purely dominant traits always beat out recessive traits.

Information Box

Even though the child in question 6 will definitely be brown-eyed, he or she will be carrying the recessive green-eyed gene from his mother. That means if he or she married someone with brown eyes (but with a recessive green-eyed gene as well), there would be a 25% chance that their child would have green eyes.

2. When two people with a pure recessive trait have a child, that child will definitely have the same recessive trait.

3. When mixed dominant and recessive traits are combined, it's anyone's guess how things will turn out.

So in question 6, then, the answer is B—the child will definitely be brown-eyed.

As for photosynthesis, that's the process in which plants use chlorophyll in order to convert sunlight into energy.

Angela: Chlorophyll is the substance that makes plants green, right?

Willy: I see you've been watching your informative afterschool specials, Angela. The main point about photosynthesis is that if you don't give plants sunlight, they die, which is why that fern that Daniel keeps in his sock drawer is quite dead.

Daniel: Oh. I thought it was my smelly socks.

Willy: Using your newfound knowledge of photosynthesis, Daniel, check out the open-response question below.

7. You have decided to grow a rubber tree. You must decide where to plant the tree in order to give it the best growing conditions. Here are the three choices you have to place the plant.

   A. in the middle of the front yard
   B. next to the side of the house where the garage is
   C. in a large pot near the window of the study

   What additional information would help you decide where to put the plant? Explain why this new information would be helpful.

This might not look like a photosynthesis question at first, but if you don't mention amount of sunlight somewhere in your answer, you won't earn a lot of points.

Angela: You know, it seems kind of like an experiment—you know, find the best place to grow this rubber tree?

Willy: That's true, Angela, and it shows that knowing how to set up an experiment properly is so important for this exam. If you don't think so, just wait until the three laboratory performance tasks: you'll be convinced by then.

To solve this open-response question, we want to come up with as many variables as we can— amount of sunlight, quality of soil, amount of rainfall, whether or not there are rubber-tree-eating animals inside or outside the house—before we decide on one of the three locations. In fact, the real question is not "Which site is best for this plant?" but "Can you figure out all the variables that go into growing a plant?" If you can answer that question, you'll do well.

Earth and Space Science

Willy: There are only two objects you need to know in order to ace this section: the earth, and the galaxy. Earth Science questions talk about minerals, the composition of soil, volcanoes, fossils, and other things that make up our little blue planet. Still, you don't need to be a vulcanologist to know that lava is hot, so be sure to use common sense whenever you can.

8. Earthquakes are most commonly associated with—

    A. faults in the earth's crust
    B. volcanoes.
    C. soil erosion.
    D. rivers and tributaries.

Willy: On a question like this, you should be thankful for the multiple-choice format. POE should help you here: D has nothing to do with the inner workings of the earth (the ground), so it can be eliminated.

Daniel: You know, I remember watching the movie Superman, and there was a lot of talk about doing something to the San Andreas Fault in order to trigger an earthquake. I'll pick A.

Willy: Cinematic knowledge aside, it would be difficult to figure out how soil erosion or volcanoes could start an earthquake. It could be done, and you could have an imaginative way of doing it, but with A, B, and C to choose from, I would pick A.

Basically, the Science test will probe your knowledge of the interconnectedness of various things (that's the name of one of the Standards, so this shouldn't be surprising). In biology, it's the cycles of organisms. In earth sciences, it's the relationship between air-water-sunlight-earth. Overall, if you apply a little common sense to the scientific knowledge you have, you should get through parts A and B of Session 1 fairly well. Together, these two parts make up 50–70% of your overall score, which means that by the time you finish all the easier questions and jump into the long, open-response questions of part C, you'll have already determined most of your final score.

Angela: That's good . . . I think.

Daniel: It is good, Angela, since it means that the bulk of your grade will be determined by multiple-choice and short open-response questions. The harder open-response questions will certainly affect your score, but not by such a massive amount.

Willy: That's right. Just answer the questions as best you can, write all your work down, and don't get flustered if you come across a very difficult problem.

Once you've finished the two-hour written test, 85 percent of your Science score has been determined. The remaining 15 percent will be determined by the one-hour laboratory portion., which is divided into three performance tasks, each 15 minutes in length. For 2001, the Laboratory Performance Tasks were:

- **Task A: Sorting Creatures**

  Organize and classify a collection of objects

- **Task B: Ramp and Golf Ball Game**

  Roll a golf ball down a ramp and collect various data

- **Task C: Woods and Water**

  Use measuring equipment to determine the properties of sample pieces of wood.

Now, each year the performance tasks will change, so don't go into this part of the test expecting to do the tasks listed above. What won't change from year to year is the focus of the test.

Look, let's be honest: The laboratory portion is trippy, because weighing pieces of wood and comparing densities is a strange thing to do for a test. However, if you go into the test knowing that unusual things might be asked of you, and that this section only accounts for 15 percent of your score, you can do well.

> **Strategy**
>
> *The laboratory tasks will require you to apply scientific methods, such as collecting data about the rolling ball. If you learn to properly use a microscope, balanced scale, and ruler, it won't matter what the actual task is; you should do well.*

If you're directed to roll a ball and collect data, then do it. If you're asked to make a graph of the results, then make a graph. It's just like making a graph for the math test.

Angela: What if a questions asks me to draw a cell, but I know I don't draw very well?

Willy: Hey, it's not an art test, it's a science test. Put down whatever you can, as well as you can. If nothing else, an aggressive approach to completing the various tasks should help you garner partial credit.

That concludes the discussion of the Science test. Now let's talk briefly about a similarly themed exam, the Technology test.

Technology Assessment Test

Willy: Well, if it isn't science, it's technology.

Daniel: What's the difference between science and technology?

Willy: Well, the answer to that can be fairly lengthy, so I'm going to answer a different question instead: What's the difference between the Grade 8 Science test and the Technology Assessment test? The Science test has more consequences for you than does the Technology test.

So don't spend time studying for this exam when you could be improving your math or ELA skills.

Angela: I know the Technology score won't count in our school district, but it might count in other school districts, right?

Willy: Yes, there's no state law requiring additional instruction if you do badly on this test, but that doesn't mean a local district or school couldn't decide to assign extra work to failing students.

In the spirit of caution, then, here is a breakdown of the Technology test.

Overview: NYS 8th Grade Technology Assessment test*

Part I	40 multiple-choice questions
Part II	10 open-response questions
Time	90 minutes total

* Though the test is usually given to eighth graders, some seventh graders can take it as well.

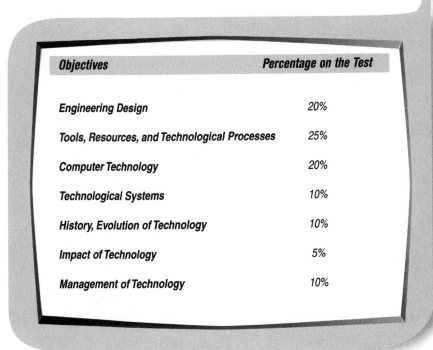

Objectives	Percentage on the Test
Engineering Design	20%
Tools, Resources, and Technological Processes	25%
Computer Technology	20%
Technological Systems	10%
History, Evolution of Technology	10%
Impact of Technology	5%
Management of Technology	10%

Willy: As you can see, no *one* category stands out, and every content strand contains a huge amount of knowledge. For example, the History and Evolution of Technology could be a 1,100 page book, and yet it accounts for only 10 percent of the test.

Trying to study each of these categories would take a great deal of time, and you still might not learn all the facts required to answer all the questions. Instead, I suggest applying the test-taking strategies you have already learned—pacing, the two-pass system—along with a healthy dose of common sense. Together, that should get you through the Technology test with a decent score.

Chapter 6

Social Studies

Session Leader: Daniel Bryant

O Herodotan One, we started a bit late for our sixth meeting. We were going to meet at the downtown library's conference room, but it turns out that last year Willy had volunteered to "improve" their fire extinguishers, and after the "foam incident" he has been asked never to set foot inside the library again. Fortunately, there was a coffeshop across the street, and while the group drank hibiscus teas—a hideous concoction—I was able to munch on some Styrofoam cups.

—X!Frumious

NAME: Daniel Bryant

ADDITIONAL NOTES: While taking standardized tests remains his hobby of choice, Daniel is also an enthusiast of history. This has helped him win the "Most Accurate Yet Obscure Costume" prize at Eastbury's Halloween party for several years. Recent costumes have included: Millard Fillmore, 13th president of the United States; renowned Roman statesman Pliny the Elder; and hallowed French physicist Marie Curie. Daniel has watched all the documentaries produced by Ken Burns so often that he can now quote large passages about the Civil War from memory.

Ridley: So what exactly did you do to those fire extinguishers, Willy?

Willy: Well, I did refill them for free, something that the librarians tend to forget when discussing the Flaming Biographies incident. But I guess I also accidentally increased their "firing range" in the process, so when Ms. Baba used one, the foam shot out about 50 feet. I guess she wasn't quite expecting that.

Angela: That story is certainly one for the history books.

Daniel: Speaking of history . . .

Overview: NYS 8th Grade Social Studies test

	Percentage of test
Session 1	
* 45 multiple-choice questions	50%
* 3 or 4 constructed-response questions	20%
Session 2	
* 6-8 scaffolding questions	10%
* 1 essay	20%

Time 90 minutes each session

Note: The constructed-response and scaffolding questions are basically short fill-in-the-blank questions. For the remainder of this chapter, they will both be referred to as short-answer questions.

Daniel: Now, the Social Science test debuted in 2001, so it's impossible to talk about any trends in the test. I can't say that NYSED features a certain type of question every year since there's been only one administration. Still, if you have an idea of the test's format, you can use the appropriate test-taking strategies when needed.

As with the other subject tests, doing the easier questions first is the way to a better score. So in session 1 of the Social Studies test, answer all the multiple-choice questions before tackling the short answers problems. In session 2, get the short-answer problems out of the way before hitting the essay.

Angela: That sounds familiar.

Daniel: Yes, in fact, you'll see that you can use many of the same strategies on the Social Studies exam that you use on the other subject tests. Here are some of them:

1. As on the Science test, you won't always need to know the exact historical (or scientific) fact in order to get a problem right.

2. As on the Math test, you'll use basic strategies to read and analyze charts and graphs.

3. As on the ELA test, you'll apply your writing skills to some of the open-response questions.

4. As on all the subject tests, POE is still your friend.

Daniel: Having told you of the similarities, let me mention an important difference that the Social Studies test has with the other tests. While POE is useful here, you will need to have some factual knowledge of history. This is similar to the Science test, but since most of us know something about basic scientific phenomena like sunlight and electricity, you could get through the science questions with relative ease. That's not always the case with history—some of us have no idea who wrote the Bill of Rights, and no amount of everyday experience will help us bridge that gap. I call this Daniel's Rule of History: In order to do well on the Social Studies exam, you'll have to know the difference between *George Washington, George Clooney,* and *Curious George,* the lovable monkey.

O Brachiating Poobah, as a being from another planet, I didn't know the difference between these three individuals, and believe me, it caused me trouble. I kept watching reruns of ER, hoping to see a monkey perform surgery.

You've got to have a good grasp of the basics, and then you can use POE and other techniques to get the right answer. Throughout this chapter I'll recommend key facts that everyone should be familiar with.

The Social Studies exam is designed to test you on a wide range of historical events; basically, most events that occurred in the last 3,000 years are up for grabs.

Ridley: Are we going to review all that? I have a curfew, you know.

Daniel: No, Ridley, I don't think that would be an efficient use of our time. This is one reason why the Social Studies test is harder to prepare for than most of the other tests: There's just so much information that could be on the test, that trying to study all of it would be a massive undertaking.

At the very least, you should familiarize yourself with the biggest events in American history. These include the four major wars America has fought: the *American Revolution*, the *Civil War*, and *World Wars I and II*.

Angela: Why the emphasis on wars? That's seems a little violent.

Daniel: Granted, wars aren't pleasant, but when you think about our country, those four events have had a huge impact on our lives. This is the type of question you could see:

> 1. During the American Revolution, which country was the biggest ally of the American colonies?
>
>   A. France
>   B. England
>   C. Mexico
>   D. Spain

If you know anything about the American Revolution, you should be able to cross out B. After that, you need to know enough about that war to know that France was our biggest ally.

Let's say you knew the basic fact that France was our biggest ally. Here's how you could use that information to answer a tougher problem.

> 2. Of the following individuals, who was the greatest ally to the United States?
>
>   A. General Cornwallis
>   B. Marquis de Lafayette
>   C. Benedict Arnold
>   D. Juan Velasquez

Willy, which answer choice has the French name?

Willy: Choice B, and since I know that France was our greatest ally, I should pick B.

Daniel: Right. Another thing you should know about session 1 of this test is that many questions come with an illustration or chart. That's good news, since what that means is that the historical facts are provided in the question itself.

3. The shaded portion of the map shows the

A. Northwest Territory.

B. Louisiana Purchase.

C. Gadsden Purchase.

D. Oregon Territory.

Even if we don't know the precise answer, we can combine the map and POE and take a good guess. I know where Louisiana and Oregon are, and since neither one is near the shaded area, I can cross out B and D. That leaves A and C, and since the shaded area is not in the northwest portion of the United States, I'll go with C.

Information Box

If a question contains some type of visual information, it isn't there for amusement. It is usually the key you'll need to answer a question correctly.

Now, as for the short-answer questions and essay, many students will worry about these more than the multiple-choice questions. That's because many people have the impression that essay questions are harder than most other problems. Well, that's true, but you should know that the essay counts for only 20 percent of your overall score. In fact, all of session 2 accounts for just 30 percent of your score. What this means is that the bulk of your grade will be determined by how well you use your test-taking skills on the multiple-choice and short-answer questions in session 1.

The format of session 2 might look familiar to you, Angela. Do you know why?

Angela: Am I featured in a full-length, tell-all reading passage?

Daniel: Not quite. However, this part of the Social Studies test is similar to the ELA exam. Session 2 starts out with 6–8 "documents," which you can think of as weird reading comprehension passages. These might be telegrams, posters, paintings, quotations, letters, invoices, or cartoons. Following each document is a short-answer question. Now where do you think the answer to that question can be found?

Angela: Within the passage, or in this case, within the document?

Daniel: That's right. Even though the format of the document might be strange, you approach the question the same way you would approach an ELA reading question. Look over the document, understand the main idea, and then refer to the passage to locate the answer.

Willy: Does that really work?

Daniel: Oh yes. To go a step further, think of every question as an Inference question: The answer isn't staring you in the face, but you have enough information to be able to figure it out.

After these questions, you'll be given one essay question. The key to a strong essay is to include the facts and information provided in the documents. As I said earlier, you'll also need some historical knowledge of your own, of course, but the documents themselves will be of great benefit.

Angela: That's just like day 2 of the ELA test, where you use the information in the passage to write your extended-response answer.

Willy: Except in this case, you're writing an essay, so you should follow the essay-writing advice I talked about.

Daniel: You're both on the money, and this just reinforces how one test-taking strategy can be used on different tests. By learning the format of the test beforehand, you give yourself a chance to prepare a plan of attack.

> O Thucydidan One, the notes were very informative, and even better tasting than Willy's soap.

Other students will go into the test just hoping to do well. You, however, can go in knowing that the proper blend of essay and reading comprehension skills will help you garner a good score on these open-ended questions.

And that's all there is to the Social Studies exam. Any questions?

X!Frumious: If you guys are done with your notes, can I have them?

Epilogue

TO: X!Frumious the Explorer, currently stationed on Earth

FROM: The Most Supreme Ruler of the planet Kronhorst

RE: Your notes about the New York State 8th Grade tests

Dear X!Frumious,

Now that I've read your notes about the New York State tests, I can easily remember why you are my favorite Kronhorstian. Thorough work! I learned quite a bit about standardized tests, and I'm quite eager to try some of those tasty charcoal briquettes you were eating earlier.

Your study group notes convinced me to learn more about these exams on my own, so I used my human Internet connection and checked out the New York State Education Department Web site at **www.nysed.gov**. It contained a wealth of information concerning the 8th Grade tests in addition to various other educational topics in New York.

I am very eager to learn how well you do on the 8th Grade exams when you take them. However, regardless of how well you do, I want you to remember that these tests are only a small part of your educational career. Getting a low score on either test doesn't mean you are a bad student—it might mean you had a bad day, or that you don't test well, or that you need to brush on some skills. So while the tests provide an interesting snapshot of your educational career, they capture only one moment and don't shed light on the full-length movie that is your entire academic career. So, if you do fail one or both of the tests, I'll speak first with the people who know your academic standing better than anyone else—your teachers there at Eastbury High. They'll be able to look over your scores and tell me how they relate to you *as a student. Until I hear from them, I will not take your test scores as any-thing more than how well you did on one set of standardized tests.*

That's all for now. Come back to Kronhorst soon—Mrs. Supreme Ruler of the planet Kronhorst misses you, as do I. If you ever need any help tutoring, drop by the palace and we'll work on some test questions together.

Stay relaxed and do the best you can on the 8th Grade exams. That's all any-one can ask from you, including me. Well, gotta go—there's a planet to run, you know. I remain

Your Loving Father,

X!Frumious, Sr.
Supreme Ruler of Kronhorst, Most Scaly One, etc.

P. S. Why don't you bring your study group over for dinner sometime?

Answer Key: Sample Questions

	Mathematics		
1.	C	12.	C
2.	C	13.	A
3.	B	14.	D
4.	D	15.	B
5.	B	16.	C
6.	D	17.	C
7.	C	18.	A
8.	A	19.	B
9.	B	20.	B
10.	D	21.	B
11.	D		

22. Mr. Grubeck's class has been collecting data of rainfall in New York. The table below shows the amount of rain for seven New York cities in August 2001.

Part A

$$\frac{14.9 + 28.6 + 35.9 + 8.4 + 16.5 + 17.5 + 2.1}{7 \text{ cities}} = 17.7 \text{ centimeters}$$

Part B

$17.5 - 4.8 = 12.7$ centimeters. Since 17.5 is 4.8 centimeters **greater** than the average rainfall, to find the average you must **subtract** 4.8 from 17.5.

Part C

Wetter. While four out of seven cities had drier months (as evidenced by the negative signs), the average rainfall difference was:

$$\frac{(-5.8) + 12.6 + 18.4 + (-0.5) + (-0.2) + 4.8 + (-2.0)}{7 \text{ cities}} = +3.9 \text{ centimeters}$$

Since the number is positive, the average rainfall was wetter.

23. What percent of the rectangle is shaded?

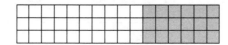

To convert a fraction to a percent, multiply that fraction by 100%.

$$\frac{3}{8} = \frac{3}{8} \times 100\% = \frac{3}{2} \times 25\% = 37\frac{1}{2}\%$$

or 37.5%

24. In the expression $\frac{4 \times 15 + 2^2 - 4}{3 - 2 \times 6}$, let's insert these two sets of parentheses which will make the expression equal to 12.

$$\frac{4 \times (15 + 2^2) - 4}{(3 - 2) \times 6}$$

Remember the order of operations, PEMDAS, which stands for Parenthe-ses, Exponents, Multiplication, Division, Addition, Subtraction. First do what's inside the parentheses, doing the exponent before the addition in $15 + 2^2$:

$$= \frac{4 \times (15 + 4) - 4}{1 \times 6}$$

$$= \frac{4 \times 19 - 4}{1 \times 6}$$

$$= \frac{76 - 4}{6}$$

$$= \frac{72}{6}$$

$$= 12$$

English Language Arts

1.	D
2.	C
3.	A
4.	C
5.	B
6.	D
7.	B
8.	Even though Du Bois and Washington both fought to improve the lives of African Americans, they had different approaches. Du Bois thought that if the more educated African Americans spoke out frequently, racism would eventually be eliminated. Washington felt that the only way to eliminate racism was for African Americans to gain economic independence. Since both men believed so strongly in their views, and because those views placed responsibility on different things, they were highly critical of each other.
9.	D
10.	B
11.	A
12.	B
13.	C
14.	A
15.	D
16.	The Panama Canal took ten years to complete. Some of the causes for its delay were tropical diseases, inadequate digging tools, and insufficient money. Once those things were under control, though, the Canal was delayed even further when the United States tried to take control of the project. Eventually, after even more disease and rat infestation, the canal was finished.
17.	Dr. William Gorgas helped to establish a disease-free environment during the building of the Panama Canal. W. E. B. Du Bois helped to establish equal rights for African Americans. Both men were pioneers in their struggles, working alone against enormous challenges. The challenges that Gorgas faced were mostly physical and environmental; the challenges that Du Bois faced were mostly social and political. But they both fought to establish better conditions for mankind.
18.	C
19.	A
20.	C
21.	B
22.	A
23.	D
24.	From 9:00 to 4:00, the Throckmorton Fine Arts Fair will display sculptures on the east lawn, and paintings in the Merriweather and Phlox Rooms. Refreshments will be available all day long, and a barbeque lunch will be served at 12:00 noon.